# The Houses of

# McKim, Mead & White

# The Houses of McKim, Mead & White

Samuel G. White

Photographs by Jonathan Wallen

Rizzoli
NEW YORK

In association with The Museums at Stony Brook

Title page: Rosecliff,
Newport, Rhode Island.

*The Houses of McKim, Mead & White* is published in association
with The Museums at Stony Brook in conjunction with the exhibition
*Stanford White on Long Island*
4 July – 1 November 1998

This publication is supported by a grant from
Furthermore, the publication program of the J. M. Kaplan Fund

First published in 1998 by
Rizzoli International Publications, Inc.
300 Park Avenue South
New York, NY 10010

Library of Congress Cataloging-in-Publication Data
White, Samuel G.
     The houses of McKim, Mead & White / Samuel G. White ; photographs
  by Jonathan Wallen.
          p.    cm.
     "Published in association with the Museums at Stony Brook in conjunction
  with the exhibition 'Stanford White on Long Island' 4 July–1 November 1998."
     Includes index and bibliographical references.
     ISBN 0-8478-2071-8
     1. McKim, Mead & White.  2. Architecture, Domestic—United States.
  3. Eclecticism in architecture—United States.  4. Architecture, Modern—
  19th century—United States.  5. Architecture, Modern—20th century—
  United States.    I. Museums at Stony Book.  II. Title.
     NA 7207.W55     1998
     728'.0973'09034—dc21                                    98-5673
                                                                CIP

Designed by Marcus Ratliff
Printed and bound in Italy

# Acknowledgments

THIS BOOK OWES its substance to the owners and curators of some thirty-five extraordinary houses and the descendants of their original builders. I hope that the celebration of those houses in this book is compensation for their generous hospitality, their cheerful accommodation, and ultimately for their seemingly limitless patience.

Any investigation into the work of McKim, Mead & White stands on the shoulders of Leland Roth's scholarship, and this effort is no exception. This book also reflects the generosity of a number of experts in the field of architecture and decorative arts: Paul Miller of the Preservation Society of Newport County; Mosette Broderick of New York University; Mary Beth Betts of the New-York Historical Society; and Janet Parks and Dan Kany of the Avery Architectural and Fine Arts Library at Columbia University.

The photography for the book and the concurrent exhibition *Stanford White on Long Island* at The Museums at Stony Brook was supported by Furthermore, the publication program of the J. M. Kaplan Fund. I am most grateful to Joan Davidson for her interest in the project. My partners, Ted Burtis and Harry Buttrick, provided material support through the office of Buttrick White & Burtis.

I cannot imagine a more talented or compatible group of professionals than those who collaborated with me. David Morton, architecture editor at Rizzoli, conceived of a book about the houses of McKim, Mead & White and willed me into being as its author. Jonathan Wallen took all of the photographs; Marcus Ratliff created the elegant design; Lara Thrasher at Buttrick White & Burtis and Robin Key at Rizzoli provided invaluable support. I thank them all. The actual closure between initial conception and the completed product was accomplished by my wife, Elizabeth White, associate publisher at Rizzoli. This book is a testament to her mastery over every single component of the project from start to finish, and I am proud to acknowledge her contribution.

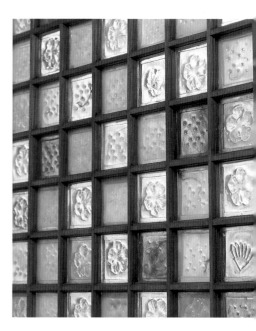

# Contents

# Introduction

ECAUSE THE SINGLE-FAMILY HOUSE is an icon of our culture, we know the names of architects who have designed famous houses. Our awareness of individual members of the design profession is more likely to center around their role in the creation and embellishment of shelter than to acknowledge their contributions to the architecture of capitalism, scholarship, or democracy. That dichotomy is particularly true of McKim, Mead & White, who transformed America's largest cities with banks, libraries, museums, and government buildings at the same time that the partners were designing the elaborate residences for which they are best known today.

This high level of "brand recognition" obscures significant artistic distinctions within the firm's work, to say nothing of its underlying quality and overall importance to American architecture. Ironically, this oversight is nowhere more true than with their residential portfolio itself. The attribution of any house to McKim, Mead & White evokes images of America's Gilded Age, and further consideration of architectural achievement is often eclipsed by social and economic history of a sensational order. In truth no building can ever be fully evaluated outside of the cultural context leading to its creation, and any account of McKim, Mead & White will invariably be accompanied by corroborative detail about the more glamorous aspects of late nineteenth century practice. But the art of architecture is realized in a physical and tangible dimension, and as works of art the houses of McKim, Mead & White constitute a portfolio of some of the most original and well-crafted designs produced in America.

The collaboration of Charles Follen McKim (1847–1909), William Rutherford Mead (1846–1928), and Stanford White (1853–1906) was established in 1879. McKim was the original leader by virtue of his education, his ability, and his clients. He had attended Harvard and the Ecole des Beaux-Arts in Paris, and had apprenticed for two years in New York with Henry Hobson Richardson at 57 Broadway before setting up his own practice

River elevation of Hyde Park, built for Frederick W. Vanderbilt, 1895–99, Hyde Park, New York.

down the hall from Gambrill & Richardson's office. Mead, the oldest of the three, was a graduate of Norwich University and Amherst College. He had apprenticed for three years with Russell Sturgis, whose office was also at 57 Broadway. In 1871 Mead left New York for two years in Florence, after which he joined McKim. Beginning in 1877 McKim and Mead were in partnership with William Bigelow, a classmate of McKim's from the Beaux-Arts and the brother of his wife Annie. McKim, Mead & Bigelow disbanded shortly after Annie Bigelow abandoned McKim in 1878.

When McKim left Gambrill & Richardson in 1872, his position as Richardson's principal assistant was immediately filled by Stanford White, a nineteen-year-old firebrand whose original plan to become an artist had been redirected into architecture. White stayed in Richardson's office until 1878, when he departed for a self-guided tour of Europe. Abroad for fifteen months, he was based in Paris in the company of American sculptor Augustus Saint-Gaudens, his lifelong friend with whom he was already collaborating on three commissions. White returned to New York in September 1879 to join McKim and Mead, forming an association that would last until their deaths.

McKim, White, and Mead each brought specific and identifiable strengths to the partnership. McKim was a designer with a keen understanding of early American buildings and decorative arts, a powerful ability to simplify forms, and a list of clients and connections that would benefit the firm for the next thirty years. White was a skilled artist, capable of creating elegant details and brilliant arrangements of texture, color, and objects based on unconventional juxtapositions. Mead ran the office and, in his own words, "kept [his] partners from making damn fools of themselves." It would be misleading to spend too much effort sorting out their individual contributions on specific projects and incorrect to see their work as anything less than a collaboration. McKim, Mead & White's architecture rose to the level of excellence because the strengths and weaknesses of each partner complemented the others, because each architect understood his own role in the process, and because they worked together. Individually, Charles Follen McKim, William Rutherford Mead, and Stanford White might have been interesting footnotes in the history of late-nineteenth-century American architecture. By their collaboration, they defined it.

During the period between 1879 and 1912, McKim, Mead & White became the largest and most important architecture office in America, if not in the world. With a staff that grew to over one hundred, the firm became the model for the modern architectural practice. In order to manage multiple large commissions, they established procedures for controlling every stage and detail of the architectural process. During its first thirty years the firm received and executed nearly one thousand commissions, championed the movement to introduce classical order to America's cities, trained the next generation of American architects, created standards of conduct for professional practice in this country, and were awarded, through McKim, the Gold Medal of the Royal Institute of British Architects.

It is virtually impossible to overstate the degree to which McKim, Mead & White dominated the business of American architecture at the turn of the century. Their clients included the period's most prominent institutions, including the Boston Public Library in 1887 and Symphony in 1892, multiple commissions for Harvard University beginning in 1889 and the plan for Columbia University in 1893, leadership in the overall planning and design of major portions of the World's Columbian Exposition of 1893, participation on the Senate Park Commission for the improvement of the Washington Mall in 1901 and renovations to the White House in 1902, and the plan for the Brooklyn Museum in 1893 as well as the expansion of the Metropolitan Museum of Art in 1904. The Newport Casino, which was among their very first projects, established the young firm in Newport at the instant of that fabled resort's explosive growth. They would later build America's first country club at Shinnecock Hills on Long Island in 1892, and they achieved a near-monopoly on the design of private clubhouses in New York.

Their work appealed to the businessman as well as to the civic-minded philanthropist and club man. Commercial commissions included Madison Square Garden in 1887, New York's Pennsylvania Station in 1902, Tiffany & Company in 1903, and The National City Bank in 1904. Commissions for non-architectural projects included monuments, picture frames, and book covers, principally designed by Stanford White. This impressive list reflected considerable artistic and organizational abilities, as well as the firms's good luck to participate in the nation's general economic recovery following the Civil War. It was a large share indeed. At the turn of the century it was difficult to walk in any major American city, visit a fashionable resort, or even buy a magazine without confronting the designs of McKim, Mead & White.

If you were particularly fortunate you lived in one. Between 1879 and 1912 the firm received over three hundred residential commissions for single family houses and to a far lesser extent for small apartments and attached dwellings, representing just under 40 percent of their total client list for that period. Approximately one hundred of their residential designs survive.

Most of the commissions came from the northeastern and mid-western United States, centering around major cities and principal resorts, but a few houses were built as far away as Texas and California. McKim, Mead & White's residential practice was an integral part of their work; house commissions defined the office and its partners—personally, artistically, and financially—at every stage of their careers.

The partners liked to design houses. McKim started out in 1872 as a house architect. By 1879 he had completed summer houses in Elberon, New Jersey, Newport, Rhode Island, and St. James, Long Island. Even after the rapid growth of the partnership, and as he became more identified with the firm's largest institutional and commercial commissions, McKim never abandoned his interest in creating houses for the American landscape. The first and last projects in this book reflect his fascination with the formal archetype of the shingled, wood-framed house under a simple gable roof. Mead is identified with fewer house commissions, and in those cases he acted as administrative partner in collaboration with one of the two design principals.

Stanford White started out seven years behind McKim, but he eventually became the partner in charge of most residential commissions. White was a better draftsman as well as a more facile and intuitive designer than McKim, and he was not wedded to a single formal paradigm. He saw houses, including their contents, their owners, and even their occupancy, as scenographic elements in the performance of life. Believing that an architect should live better than his clients, White was the only one of the three partners to maintain elaborate country and city residences. He extended the traditional limits of architectural services to include interior decoration, dealing in art and antiques, and even planning and designing parties. In spite of White's virtuosity, and possibly because of it, some of the firm's clients preferred the diffident McKim or the even more businesslike Mead, and many were at least wary of White's reputation for sacrificing the stated budget for the sake of the final effect. Nonetheless, in these transactions, White had an advantage over his partners: he got along well with everyone.

---

TAKEN TOGETHER AND ORDERED chronologically, the houses of McKim, Mead & White illustrate the development of the firm as well as the changing times at the turn of the century. All houses can be classified according to three principal phases—early, transitional, and mature, and each phase is marked by a distinct style. The basis for the distinguishing characteristics of each phase and style lie in a combination of social and architectural

forces that were initiated beyond the walls of the office, as well as in the evolving careers and distinctive personalities of the partners.

The firm's earliest work is characterized by imagination and experimentation and suggests a high degree of collaboration between the individual partners. As young architects, the majority of their commissions were for country houses. These were designed as wood-framed structures with relatively simple forms recalling the architecture of eighteenth-century New England. Because they were built of materials most vulnerable to aging, because low construction costs permitted large structures, and because there was a period when their artistic qualities were underappreciated, most of the early houses have been lost, including three of the best, the H. Victor Newcomb house in Elberon, New Jersey (1880), the Cyrus R. McCormick house in Richfield Springs, New York (1880–82), and the William G. Low house in Bristol, Rhode Island (1886–87). The image of the Low house with its massive single gable covering all the irregularities of the house below has become an icon of American architecture.

The basic characteristics of the early country houses are well illustrated by each of these lost masterpieces. They were vacation houses, built for middle-class professionals or first-generation entrepreneurs to accommodate the relatively novel phenomenon of leisure time. Their architectural vocabulary followed a formula that permitted a wide variety of expression. The volume of the house supported a simple, gabled roof. Exterior surfaces were usually covered with raw shingles on the upper walls and roof and unpainted clapboard below. Siding and trim were wrapped tightly around the volume of the house and arranged in lively patterns. There were generous porches, occasional towers or bay windows, and frequent use of screens to break up light and shadow, but no projecting eaves or drips to diffuse the crisp edges and continuous surface of wall and roof. Double-hung, multi-paned windows, bundled in irregularly spaced groups and set flush to the wall, extended the effect of a taut, patterned skin stretched over the volume of the structure.

Left to right:
H. Victor Newcomb house, Elberon, New Jersey, 1880.

Cyrus R. McCormick house, Richfield Springs, New York, 1880–82.

William G. Low house, Bristol, Rhode Island, 1886–87.

Charles L. Tiffany
New York, 1882–85.

The effect was of simple, solid geometry organized into bold contrasts of solid and void, with an animated, textured surface that celebrated the play of light.

The interiors of all the early houses were planned with great freedom. They were arranged around a large central circulation space called a living hall, which typically featured an extra-wide front door, generous fireplace, broad staircase, and built-in bench or inglenook. Space flowed horizontally in all directions through tall pocket doors and wide openings, which permitted easy connections from room to room, and, in the case of the country houses, from indoors to outdoors. Daylight, introduced by large and freely spaced windows glazed with plate and blown glass in a variety of configurations, was suffused with color, fragmented by wooden screens, and released to play all over surfaces that ranged from highly reflective to absorptive. Interior decoration and furnishings anticipated the ascendancy of the arts and crafts movement over the previous decades' preference for Gothic. The most elaborate rooms revealed undercurrents of the emerging fashion for oriental motifs.

The early country houses synthesized experiments from earlier projects by Richardson as well as by McKim and his contemporaries in Boston and Philadelphia. The country houses in particular represented a significant advance in the development of a true American style, a theme that had obsessed avant-garde architects and that reached a crescendo around the 1876 Centennial Exposition in Philadelphia. At the time of their construction the architects referred to these houses as "modern colonial," but Vincent Scully subsequently christened them with the more evocative "shingle style."

From the very beginning of their partnership the firm designed houses for the city as well as for the country. Compared to the country houses, the early town houses reveal a more restless search for an appropriate expression on the facade even though they were built of masonry, a material that would suggest greater limitations than wood. The triple townhouse they built for Charles L. Tiffany (1882–85) says more about White's European travels than it does about McKim's vision for the ideal city, and it says even more about the lasting influence of their mutual employer and mentor, H. H. Richardson. Realized as a wholly original collage of medieval vignettes set below a monumental gable, it suggests that the model for building out the empty blocks of New York would be found in the homes of the burghers of Lille or Bruges. The block of six town houses for Henry Villard (1882–85), their most significant early town house design, illustrates the disciplined urban-

ism that the partners would eventually champion even while they continued to experiment with alternatives to the understatement of the Italian
Renaissance.

Left: Charles J. Osborn
house, Mamaroneck,
New York, 1883–85.

Right: H. A. C. Taylor house,
Newport, Rhode Island,
1884–86.

---

FOLLOWING THE SUCCESS of their early seaside cottages, the young firm
received commissions for other types of houses in other locations, for which
shingled villas in the modern colonial style were not always appropriate.
Winter occupancy, inland sites, and the elevated cultural aspirations of richer
clients encouraged by a continued rise in the national economy, all seemed
to justify the expression of a more permanent investment in home-building.
This is one explanation for the greater use of masonry and the appearance of
more academically "correct" styles ranging from Norman and Queen Anne
to aspiring neoclassical, as seen in their country houses for Charles J. Osborn
(1883–85), Mrs. Mark Hopkins (1885–86), and H. A. C. Taylor (1884–86).
Built for the son of one of McKim's first clients, the Taylor house was originally conceived in brick. While the last minute change to wood may appear
to be a regression to the firm's earlier seaside houses, its realization in a high
Georgian style anticipates the formality of their mature designs.

This transitional period lasted from 1883 to 1891, overlapping the
firm's early and later work. The houses designed during this phase are characterized by an exceptionally broad range of images, suggesting a search for
a new paradigm on the part of the clients as well as their architects. This
period was also one of great personal change for the three partners, and one
that would cause them to reevaluate their attitudes towards the design of
houses. Between February 1884 and June 1885 White, Mead, and McKim
all married.

Top: Hamilton F. Twombley house, Florham, Madison, New Jersey, 1890–1900

Above: Clarence Mackay house, Harbor Hill, Roslyn, Long Island, 1899–1902

But as Wayne Andrews explained in *Architecture, Ambition, and Americans,* the most significant development of McKim, Mead & White's transitional period was not occurring in their cramped offices at 57 Broadway, but a few blocks away in the offices of their older and more established competitor, Richard Morris Hunt. Working for the children and grandchildren of Commodore Cornelius Vanderbilt in the early and mid-1880s, Hunt looked at the palaces of European nobility as inspiration for the houses of America's richest family. After identifying an appropriate prototype, he freely modified it to fit the site and the client's program, and surrounded it with a landscape that helped even the dimmest observer to understand the connection between the provenance of the original model and social status of the current occupants.

ONCE AMERICA's other plutocrats saw how a Vanderbilt lived, they wanted more of the same. Matching the dramatic shift in their market with an equally nimble response, McKim, Mead & White redirected the their residential practice. In 1890 they began to design vast country houses in a Georgian vocabulary for two Vanderbilt sons-in-law, Hamilton F. Twombley and Elliott Fitch Shepard, and in January 1891 they began collaborating on plans for the 1893 world's fair. Since the Vanderbilt houses took several years to build, McKim, Mead & White's new paradigm had its debut in the plaster and lath pavilions of the World's Columbian Exposition in Chicago.

The imperial formality of the grand houses masks designs of considerable sophistication. McKim, Mead & White transformed generic models for classical temples and western European palaces into original compositions to fit unique sites and programs. They had to balance their client's requirements for image and program with their own high standards for composition, proportion, and ornament. They had to accommodate, seamlessly and invisibly, the increasingly complex systems for structure, ventilation, electricity, plumbing, and elevators. Late projects such as Clarence Mackay's Harbor Hill (1899–1902) married the architectural vocabulary and social ambitions of the Maisons Lafitte with the mechanics and operations of a modern battleship.

While many of the houses of this period are derived from a variety of European sources, there were significant exceptions. The partners' long-standing interest in American architecture of the previous century, combined with their appreciation of simple massing and elegant detail, led to the development of two considerably more native paradigms. Houses for Edwin

Dennison Morgan in Wheatley Hills (1890–91 and 1898–1900) and for John Howard Whittemore in Middlebury (1894–96) illustrate their colonial revival style for country houses. Shingled and clapboard forms roofed with simple gables and slightly more complex gambrels are decorated with classical moldings at the eaves and window surrounds, balconies with console brackets and urn-shaped balusters, and porches with fluted columns, all picked out with white paint. Double-hung six-over-six windows are set in regularly punched openings, and oversized dutch doors at the principal entrances are flanked by elegantly leaded sidelights and fanlights. This elastic vocabulary, combining elements of the strictly Yankee shingle style with the cultivated mannerisms of the neo-Grec, has continued to decorate country houses for the past one hundred years and constitutes one of McKim, Mead & White's most amiable contributions to the American landscape.

The firm's urban equivalent of their colonial revival house was a revival of the federal style town house. Based on the Boston designs of Charles Bulfinch and the Salem houses of Samuel McIntire, McKim, Mead & White's numerous exercises in this style employ elegant brickwork in soft colors with white marble trim, classical entrance porches, Georgian ironwork, and double-hung sash with divided lights. The partners knew this style in its original form through their early sketching expeditions and later through the firm's significant presence in New England. Their own designs in the federal style ranged from the typical New York rowhouse such as their residence for Charles Dana Gibson (1902–03), to the sophisticated resolution of an oblique Washington corner demonstrated by their house for Thomas Nelson Page (1896–97). The Anglo-American origins of these facades represented a departure from European prototypes, and the selection of such a deceptively simple aesthetic may have signified an unusual degree of social and cultural self-confidence on the part of the clients. Today McKim, Mead & White's federal style town houses epitomize the permanence and modesty of civilized taste.

In addition to the trend towards more formal designs with a greater degree of archeological correctness, the work of their mature period is characterized by an increasing tendency towards restraint in the application of color, ornament, and form. The flamboyance of the earlier houses—expressed in picturesque asymmetry and dramatic contrasts of solid and void, thick and thin, rough and smooth—is replaced by an extremely high level of discipline. Houses and landscapes are resolved as expressions of symmetry, harmony, and classical balance however irregular the site or top-heavy the program. Late designs such as the Joseph Pulitzer house, Rosecliff, and The

Top: John Howard Whittemore house, Middlebury, Connecticut, 1894–96.

Above: Edwin Dennison Morgan III house, Wheatley Hills, Long Island 1890–91 and 1898–1900.

Orchard create powerful and fully coordinated images that exceed in overall effect what the earlier designs achieved through theatrical contrasts and sheer inventiveness.

---

BECAUSE MOST ARCHITECTURE begins with a commission, architects are influenced by the period in which they work at least as much as they exert an influence on that period. The houses of McKim, Mead & White reflected as well as initiated profound changes in American architecture. Their early designs made their debut in a time and place with the triple benefits of a rising economy, the services of a growing architectural profession, and an emerging interest in national identity. Domestic interest in classical architecture had waned by the middle of the nineteenth century. In the decades prior to 1880 the new developments in American countryside featured expressions in Gothic, Anglo-Italianate, and French mansarded styles, an effect that is still visible in entire areas such as Block Island and Oak Bluffs on Martha's Vineyard. In other places this picturesque if slightly formulaic architecture was swept aside by shingle style cottages, whose builders favored its planning convenience, capacity for regional expression, and simple novelty. Following the completion of the Newport Casino, suburbs and resorts were rapidly filled with highly original buildings created by a host of able contemporaries such as Babb, Cook & Willard in New York, Peabody & Stearns and William Ralph Emerson in Boston, and Wilson Eyre in Philadelphia. The firm's subsequent evolution into more formal styles similarly anticipated and reflected a corresponding shift in popular taste nationwide. McKim, Mead & White abandoned the shingle style not long after they developed it, but they were not alone. Today America's best preserved boulevards are filled with grand houses by other architects, working in styles ranging from freestyle French provincial to high neoclassic which were employed and refined during the firm's transitional and mature phases.

Ironically the full impact of the houses of McKim, Mead & White had the least effect on the firm itself. Following the deaths of White and McKim, residential projects virtually disappeared from the firm's portfolio. William Mitchell Kendall, the most forceful and probably the most talented of the second generation of partners, had trained under McKim and his leadership of the office over the next thirty years reflected McKim's professionalism, academicism, and preference for institutional clients, without a trace of the founding partners' passion for houses. Under Kendall the firm completed houses in New York for Thomas Newbold (1916–18), Edward T. Blair in

Chicago (1912–14), and a small number of others, but the most significant residential design after 1910 was an apartment building at 998 Fifth Avenue for the Century Holding Company. Kendall may have welcomed the commission more for its significant vertical dimension than as a chance to broaden the firm's residential practice into an emerging building type. Old habits die hard, and the granite and limestone walls of 998 possess an imperial sobriety that complements the firm's vast extension to the Metropolitan Museum of Art on the other side of Fifth Avenue. The firm never designed another apartment building, and the second generation at McKim, Mead & White missed the chance to become the innovators in high-rise dwellings that the founders had been for cottages and palaces.

That choice was the firm's loss. McKim, Mead & White's reputation as the most famous architecture office in the country carried them well into the late 1930s, but the next wave of residential design was led by a younger generation of architects who had trained with the original partners before embarking on their own. Individuals such as John Russell Pope (who modeled his professional persona on McKim) and offices led by former draftsmen such as Carrere & Hastings, Delano & Aldrich, and Harrie T. Lindeberg designed great private houses for wealthy individuals. The classical and academic aspects of McKim, Mead & White's mature houses were the common point of departure for most architects who were their direct successors. The robust spirit of innovation and experimentation in the firm's earliest houses re-emerged in the designs of a completely different strain of American architect, Frank Lloyd Wright. Vincent Scully has argued that Wright's early houses were a direct extension of the shingle style. Wright's houses for middle-class patrons reflected an underlying Jeffersonian outlook. His formal vocabulary is based on shingle style motifs including the strong horizontal movement in plan and elevation, reliance on bold contrasts, fondness for the anchoring character of the hearth, easy transitions from interior to exterior, and ornamental motifs ranging from the arts and crafts movement to Japan. To Scully, the qualities which found such a novel expression in Wright's Prairie and Usonian houses are part of a continuous development of American architecture that had its first significant expression in the early houses of McKim, Mead & White.

In the 1950s Lawrence Grant White observed that his father's best buildings had already been torn down. He was probably referring to houses for Osborn, Tiffany, and Vanderbilt, as well as to Madison Square Garden and the Madison Square Presbyterian Church, the building many consider to have been White's masterpiece. He was not counting McKim's work, which generally had a better record of survival. Stanford White's son may not have been particularly aware of the Low house in Bristol, which would disappear in the late 1960s, and could not have even contemplated the possibility of the 1963 demolition of Pennsylvania Station. The architectural record of western culture from the end of World War II to the birth of the preservation movement in the late 1960s was as significant for the appalling loss of valuable buildings as for the no less dispiriting creations of the majority of contemporary architects.

In the light of collective cultural amnesia on that scale, the survival of even one hundred of McKim, Mead & White's houses is a cause for celebration, and the nature and details of their survival are worth examining. Many are no longer houses. Of the existing houses designed between 1879 and 1912, about half remain occupied as single or multiple family dwellings, a number are preserved as house museums, and the rest are used for a variety of occupancies ranging from office space to dormitories. In general the grander the house, the more likely it is to have been converted to another use.

The houses that remain residences do so because they are still highly livable in an increasingly servant-less age. Their interiors contain welcoming halls, beautiful staircases, dignified chambers. They are generally well built, they are filled with elegant details, and there is not too much distance between the kitchen and the dining room. Some, such as the houses for the Kings, Goelets, Wetherills, and Whites, are intact because the families for whom they were built managed to sustain their progeny, property, and in some cases prosperity through the most destructive phases of the pre-preservation period. Others benefited from peculiarities of the original planning combined with a good location, none more so than the Southampton house for James Breese and the New York town house for Joseph Pulitzer, both of which have been successfully adapted to multi-family occupancy. Other survivors were just plain lucky. After years of occupancy by indifferent owners and incarnations as seaside hotels, the Tilton house and most of the Association houses have been restored as single family residences and are testaments to the extraordinary quality of the firm's earliest work.

A majority of the houses have survived through adaptation to new uses. The most natural conversion, into a house museum, usually requires the generosity of owners and survival of the original furniture. The Mills, Vanderbilt, Choate, Pope, and Oelrichs houses are museums open to the public, soon to be joined by the Bell house. The other houses are occupied as working buildings, and every one has a different story.

The Pyne house was saved from demolition by an indignant neighbor, who bought and donated it to an association promoting inter-American relations. The Villard Houses served as chancery offices for the Archdiocese of New York and the headquarters of Random House for over thirty years, enough time to gain protection from New York's Landmarks Preservation Commission. In the late 1970s the houses were restored to accommodate a restaurant, the entrance to a hotel, and offices for a collection of civic-minded organizations. The Winans house was a school, a funeral parlor, and doctors' offices until it had the great fortune to become the headquarters of a preservation-minded publishing company. Other houses have found sympathetic reincarnations ranging from corporate headquarters to main administration buildings, and the suites of rooms that originally celebrated the social ambitions of plutocrats now dignify the activities of foundations, university presidents, and corporations.

The most congenial of the conversions transformed houses into clubs, a new use that capitalizes on the stylish comfort of the original occupancy and takes advantage of the separate domains for formal activities and support services. Stanford White recognized the natural fit between the two programs when he converted Edwin Booth's New York town house into the Players Club in 1888–89, and he would have applauded the reincarnation of his houses for Elliott Fitch Shepard and Thomas Benedict Clarke into the Sleepy Hollow Country Club and the Collectors Club. The conversion to a country club entailed the construction of extensive locker facilities, and the organization for philatelists has an unusual storage requirement, but like all clubs they take advantage of the large scale and ceremonial nature of the public spaces on the lower floors. On the other hand, the transformation of the Patterson house into the Washington Club appears to have been effortless. The members play bridge in the chambers upstairs, which in most club conversions are used as offices and small meeting rooms. The most startling adaptation of the upstairs spaces is a result of population density, rather than use. On the floors where John Forrester Andrew's three children and their servants once lived, twenty-five members of Phi Chi fraternity sleep three to a room.

It is to these owners that this book is dedicated with the hope that they will be encouraged to preserve what they have already saved.

Overleaf: Dining room
at Kingscote, Newport,
Rhode Island, 1880–81.

# Prescott Hall Butler House

# Bytharbor

## St. James, Long Island
## 1878–80

rescott Hall Butler and Charles Follen McKim first met at Harvard, but their close friendship dates from the mid 1870s. Both men had recently married, and the two couples lived in the same building on Thirteenth Street in New York—"up four flights" with the McKims "separated from us by a wall," as Butler noted in his journal. Butler's wife, the former Cornelia Smith, was the eldest of five daughters of Judge J. Lawrence Smith of Smithtown, Long Island. In 1878 Butler purchased three tracts of land in nearby St. James overlooking St. James Harbor, and established a small working farm, commissioning McKim to design a cottage for his family.

The planning of the Butler house illustrates the principal problem of building on Long Island's North Shore: the entrance faces south while the view of the water is to the north. McKim's response to the site was to design a house that is just one room deep, with a highly articulated elevation facing the carriage drive and a plainer garden facade overlooking the harbor. The entire composition is dominated by the massing. The original block consists of a long, narrow gable, stretched almost beyond its natural limits to enclose the extremities of the plan below. None of McKim's previous designs displays such boldness. No other architect besides H. H. Richardson had achieved McKim's ability to simplify forms, and Richardson was working in

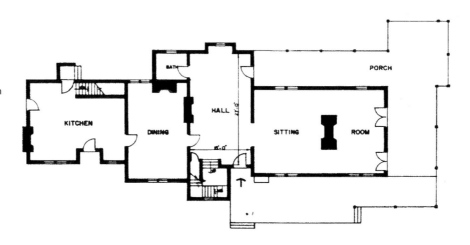

Ground floor plan. This plan represents a short-lived (and possibly unbuilt) configuration of the ground floor before the entrance hall was enlarged and the fireplace separating it from the dining room was eliminated.

The bold form of the long gable, perhaps the quintessential element of the shingle style vocabulary, makes an early appearance at Bytharbor. (Collection of The New-York Historical Society)

Today the entrance facade retains most of its original elements; the enlargement of the dining room required additional windows on the left.

The expression of interior spaces on the exterior of the house was an important shingle style element, seen here in the projection of the stairhall with its oversized window. The patterning of shingles and the use of colonial detail were typical of the early houses.

masonry. With its great gable, the Butler house represents a significant advance in the development of McKim's vocabulary for shingle style buildings, a style that dominated his work until the late 1880s. McKim would continue to revisit his paradigm for Butler's roof, perfecting it in the house designed for William G. Low (1886–87) in Bristol, Rhode Island.

Bytharbor seems modest for any significance as a precedent setter. Its front elevation is a balanced composition of asymmetrically placed rectangles set at different planes and held together by continuous horizontal lines and the overarching roof. Elements from the standard early shingle style vocabulary are assembled according to the personal grammar McKim had developed over the previous five years through his designs for houses in Elberon, New Jersey, and Newport, Rhode Island. The one-story base is clad in white painted clapboard, while the wall above is covered with an aggressive texture of notched shingles. A flair in the bottom course of shingles emphasizes the division of gable and plinth, and the roof descends almost to the ground. The upper windows are grouped to form a larger composition that is tied back into the stair bay with a bracketed cornice. The second floor corbels deeply over the entrance, sheltering its large dutch door. The porches are relatively plain, with thin square columns and simple railings. The oval window at the master bath and the scalloping in the pediments derive from McKim's interest in eighteenth-century architecture and decorative arts.

The interiors of Butler's cottage are planned with great freedom and decorated with restraint. The compact stair originally opened to a large, low hall extending the full depth of the building. A period photograph shows a columned bay window overlooking the harbor, an off-center fireplace, and a built-in cupboard. The stair is clad in vertical beaded board; the chimney is paneled in a colonial manner; and the cupboard is topped with an elaborate pediment in high Georgian style.

Bytharbor illustrates the style of McKim working on his own, revealing his ability as a simplifier of form and his interest in the architecture and furniture of colonial America. The mechanical texture of the elevations and the chaste interiors also indicate his lack of interest in elaborate finishes or ambitious decoration. After White's arrival in September 1879, work prepared in the office at 57 Broadway would have a very different look.

McKim and White would be closely allied with the Butler household throughout their lives. McKim introduced his younger partner to Cornelia Butler's sister Bessie, whom White married in 1884. Shortly thereafter the Whites began to rent and ultimately bought the land directly across the

The geometry of the small staircase with its rhetorical bottom step, implied inglenook, dowelled and panelled screens, and simple white beaded board walls is characteristic of the early work of McKim.

road from the Butlers. In succeeding years, McKim and White worked together on several projects for the family, including the design of St. Paul's Church in Stockbridge, Massachusetts, dedicated to the memory of Butler's mother, and a town house at 22 Park Avenue in New York.

Butler later retained the firm for additions to Bytharbor, a complex of barns, and a playhouse with a large ballroom. In the mid 1890s White designed a ten-story windmill, allegedly the tallest structure on Long Island. The tower, sited on Butler's land but possibly owned jointly with White, was built to pump spring water up from the harbor to their two houses at the top of the hill. The family friendships endured after the deaths of both Butler and White. The ailing McKim retired to St. James and lived in a cottage on the Butler property until his death in 1909.

Bytharbor is still a private residence, although the original plan has been significantly altered. The windmill was destroyed by fire, and the barns were demolished. The playhouse, converted to residential use, is now a separate property.

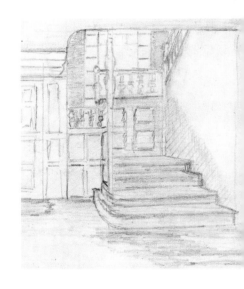

Drawing of a stair in one of McKim's sketchbooks. (Private collection)

David King Jr. House

# Kingscote

Newport, Rhode Island
Addition, 1880–81

INGSCOTE IS AMONG the earliest of approximately one thousand commissions executed by McKim, Mead & White between 1879 and 1912. If the firm had designed nothing after 1880, the dining room at Kingscote would have ensured the partners a place in the history of American interior design.

Stanford White returned from Europe on September 6, 1879 and immediately joined his friends McKim and Mead at 57 Broadway. At about the same time their client David King Jr. had acquired his family's 1841 Gothic revival house designed by Richard Upjohn at the head of Newport's Bellevue Avenue. In response to King's program for space to accommodate an escalating social life, his architects relocated the service wing and inserted a three-story addition between it and the main block of the house.

On the exterior the addition is designed as a three-story tower that retains the color scheme and some of the window details of the original house.

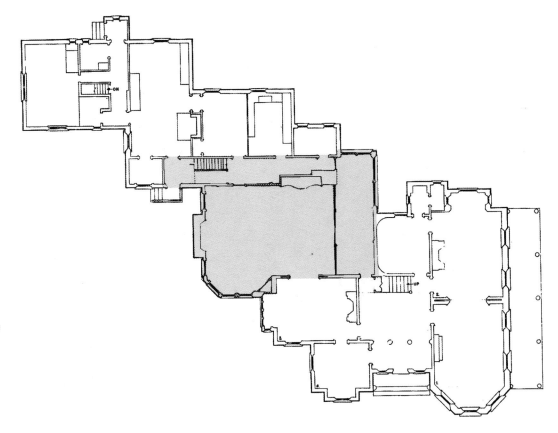

Ground floor plan. The shaded area indicates the McKim, Mead & White addition and shows how the original plan was cracked open to accommodate the new dining room. (The Preservation Society of Newport County)

The brass sconces were obtained from Archer & Pancost Mfg. Co. of New York; Louis C. Tiffany & Co. fabricated the colored glass blocks.

The project is representative of the early work of the firm in a number of ways, beginning with its location in the Northeast's principal resort. It was among the earliest of more than thirty commissions in Newport, ranging from the Casino, which the firm began in 1879, to Rosecliff, finished in 1902. In the early 1870s, McKim had spent summers in Newport, initially to court Annie Bigelow, the sister of his early partner William Bigelow, and, after their marriage in 1874, to make connections with the increasingly prosperous and highly compatible members of the summer community. The commissions McKim received in Newport prior to 1879 suggest that his practice was already established, and a significant number of the firm's later projects can be traced to connections made there.

Newport appealed to McKim's intellectual side as well. Finding the city a vanishing treasury of colonial artifacts, in 1873 he commissioned a photographic study of its older structures, interiors, and decorative arts. In the course of that enterprise he probably met Dr. David King Sr., founder of the Newport Historical Society.

As a small addition to an existing house, the Kingscote commission suggests the limited opportunities of a fledgling firm as well as the respect (and the bias) with which the partners approached the works of distinguished predecessors. The Gothic cottage was out of fashion by the late 1870s, but McKim and Mead had gained some familiarity with that aesthetic through the time they spent in the office of Russell Sturgis, who sought to create an American architecture based on the principles of Ruskin. The elevations of the Kingscote addition illustrate the tension between the young architects' respect for historic prototypes and an emerging confidence in their own style. The new design almost subordinates itself to the picturesque original, principally by its adherence to the color scheme. The difference between 1841 and 1880 is seen in the lapped shingles (instead of monolithic wood siding), the flatter angle of the tower's roof, and the non-Gothic double-hung windows. The bolder massing of the tower and chimney stands out from the nervous angularity of the earlier house, and shingle style details such as the flaring drip-line at the second story show that the addition is closer to the spirit of Richardson than that of Walpole or Scott.

While some of the trappings of the tower addition reflect the context of the Gothic house, the design is closely aligned with earlier projects of the mid-1870s by the two older partners. Mead set a similar octagon at the corner of his Cayuga Lake Hotel project while McKim folded the wings of the Francis Blake Jr. house around a tower that is the twin of the one for King.

The exterior of Kingscote may reveal a slight ambivalence of the partners

In the bay of the dining room, the play of daylight through stained glass creates a rich and ever-changing effect.

The Kingscote dining room was the first expression of the decorative virtuosity of Stanford White, who was responsible for its unusually broad range of materials and colors.

33

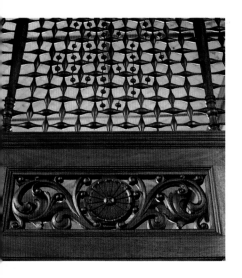

Detail of the intricately carved mahogany screen at the entrance to the dining room.

toward Gothic revival architecture, but the dining room is an accomplished work of interior design. The cramped interior of the older structure explodes in an orgy of sensuous materials, colored light, and decorated surfaces. White had spent six years working under Richardson, the first four on the tower and interiors of Trinity Church in Boston and the last two decorating the public chambers of the New York state capitol. An accomplished renderer of surface texture, and indoctrinated in the master's credo that no detail or fitting was unimportant, White is generally credited as the lead designer for the dining room itself. There is nothing in McKim's or Mead's earlier work that suggests intense interest in interiors.

The planning of the room is relatively simple: a folding screen defines an anteroom at the entrance and retracts to allow for larger parties. The pictorial vocabulary is considerably more complex, celebrating multiple qualities of light as it is reflected, transmitted, and absorbed by different materials, colors, and textures. Unfinished cork tiles in a herringbone pattern fill the squares between varnished mahogany panel strips on the ceiling. The cork runs down the upper wall to meet the high mahogany wainscoting; cherry strips pick up the same pattern at a smaller scale on the floor. Daylight penetrates stained-glass flowers and their surround of clear, blue, and green glass tiles to dissolve the wall around the mantle, itself composed of oiled black iron, yellow Siena marble, glazed celadon tiles, polished brass trim, and opalescent glass shades. An oak cornice set as a high dado holds the composition together like a belt.

The distinction between architecture and furniture is blurred by the highly finished and minutely detailed built-in cabinets, doors, and window surrounds. The expression of McKim and White's interest in American colonial decorative arts is allowed to achieve an almost oriental richness. Here the serpentine hardware and exotic light fixtures, combined with Tiffany tiles and Japanese floral motifs, reveal an omnivorous taste that places the room squarely in the aesthetic movement. Loose furnishings combine family heirlooms with oriental ceramics that reflect the Kings' colonial ancestry and their more recent success in the China trade. Stanford White found the large spinning wheel in a King barn, and persuaded his clients to use it as a foil to the stylish architectural millwork.

The King family occupied the house until 1972 when it was bequeathed to the Preservation Society of Newport County, which operates it as a house museum.

The built-in sideboard, a feature in a number of the firm's early houses, combines familiar colonial details such as the ball-and-claw foot with exotic fittings rendered in brass. King family silver and oriental ceramics are displayed on its shelves.

# Samuel Tilton House

## Newport, Rhode Island
## 1880–82

AMUEL TILTON'S ADDRESS, 12 Sunnyside Place off Beach Road, reflected the fashion of the 1870s as Newport expanded uphill from the eighteenth-century quarter that McKim had documented in his photographic survey. Beginning early in that decade the lots around Red Cross Avenue filled up with modest cottages, rendered in highly picturesque styles and occupied by professionals in the arts. Tilton was a painter who later moved to Naples where he became a dealer specializing in advising wealthy Americans on assembling collections of European art. John La Farge, painter and stained-glass window artisan, lived next door at 10 Sunnyside Place, two doors away from the 1873–74 Swiss chalet of architect and antiquarian George Champlin Mason. McKim, Mead & White was to establish a considerable presence in the district, initially through McKim's bizarre 1876–77 onion-domed residence for Katherine Prescott Wormley, at 2 Red Cross Avenue, and later through four houses designed between 1880 and 1884, all within a radius of less than one hundred yards. The last was for William G. Edgar, Commodore of the New York Yacht Club, whose sprawling brick villa had to accommodate a more ambitious social program than its middle-class neighborhood could easily support. By 1884 more astute navigators had already anticipated the shift toward Bellevue Avenue.

The elevations of the Tilton house are related to the earlier work of McKim and Mead, but at the same time they represent a significant advance. Here a far richer palette of materials and details is pressed into the service of an architecture that ranges from restless scenography to disciplined coherence. The overall effect is highly original. A two-story spindled porch, visible in old photographs, originally bisected the entrance facade. The approach to the house is now dominated by the pebbledash corner, in which a taut vertical grid of painted timbers frames panels of stucco imbedded with pebbles. The upper stories cantilever over an unusually erratic datum, established by the base of Stonington granite set in ashlar courses with coal "jewels" inserted into the mortar joints.

On the north facade, an irregular base of Stonington ashlar granite supports the cantilevered mass of the house. The walls are divided into panels of pebbledash and beveled glass.

The original entrance of the Tilton house was marked by a two-story porch. The spindled screen is similar to those used in the Newport Casino. (Collection of The New-York Historical Society)

Around the corner the architecture and materials change dramatically. The south elevation is organized into a monumental gable, framed by brick chimneys and layered into horizontal bands. Colonial crown moldings connect the heads and sills of double-hung windows, which alternate with fixed wood panels. Vertical window bays shift in and out of the shadows below the gable's deep, paneled soffit. All other surfaces are tightly wrapped in wood shingles. The shift in vocabulary from painterly and medieval to formal and classical is abrupt, but it is not absolute. Central panels are carved into sunbursts; courses of shingles are trimmed in a range of animated patterns; and even the chimney tops are decorated with sgraffito, a combination of glass, shells, and pebbles with stucco to form architectural "paintings." The split personality displayed by the two principal views of the house suggests a short-lived struggle for design control within the office. The summer houses that McKim, Mead & White built over the next five years owe more to this south elevation than to its picturesque siblings to the north and west.

The great gable of the south facade reveals the shingle style vocabulary of taut, textured surfaces, horizontal bands of windows, decorative panels, and continuous string courses. The music room is on the right.

The decorated stucco panels became a signature element in the firm's emerging shingle style, but one that they abandoned in their eventual shift to a more classical vocabulary for shingled buildings. Similar devices appear in Puritan vernacular structures, which the partners probably came across during their walking and sketching trip along the New England coast during the summer of 1877. The Tilton house has two large panels flanking the entrance, in which shards of brown and green glass are perfectly matched by the colors of the stone base and painted trim. White is said to have commandeered empty beer bottles from the workmen on the site for the "paintings," which he would then create on the spot.

The modest interior program includes an entry hall, a living room, and a dining room. The large music room may have been an afterthought, added late in the design in response to the burgeoning social life of Newport. The other rooms are relatively small, and there is no formal circulation on the ground floor other than that of the central living hall. The compactness of the plan is offset by an immense staircase, which vacuums space up to the second floor, and by the enormous window over the landing.

There is an abundance of built-in elements including mantels, wardrobes, drawers, window seats, architectural lighting, and an astonishing density of detail. Unpainted pine, the most modest of materials, is carved into fishscale capitals and pilasters, turned and doweled into spindled screens, arrayed in sunburst panels, polished into a damask of marquetry blocks,

Sunburst sgraffito panel, composed of pebbles, shells, and bottle glass, on the north facade.

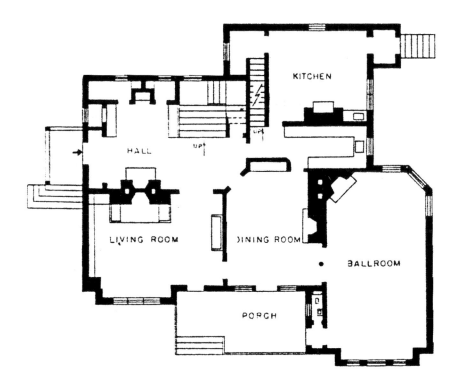

Ground floor plan.

combed to recreate the surface of rough limestone, and even coaxed to simulate burnished, upholstered leather. Leaded glass ranges from designs in cool Cartesian elegance at the stair landing and spidery calligraphy in the dining room to globules of molten glass by the front door. Gold leaf highlights ornamental details in the painted living room. Its walls were once covered with antique velvet, while the ceiling of the dining room was originally hung with fishnet.

The living room's decorative motifs combine McKim's interest in colonial furniture, expressed in the scalloped niches flanking the fireplace, with elements of Owen Jones's ornamental vocabulary. Other devices and themes reappear from the firm's earlier work. A low pulvinated frieze, a reincarnation of the Kingscote cornice, encloses the dining room as a

A double-height leaded glass window bathes the stair with light. The horizontal wooden screen at transom height became a standard part of the firm's vocabulary for interiors as well as exteriors.

The panels of the dutch door at the entry are decorated with blocks of pine, cut to expose the endgrain.

A pair of pocket doors separates the dining room from the music room beyond. Columns and pilasters throughout the house belong to an imaginary order characterized by carved fishscales.

protean belt course, becoming in turns the high chair rail, the low mantel, and the upper drawers in a built-in sideboard. Doweled panels, spindled plate rails, and open rosettes are copied from Moroccan architecture and French provincial furniture.

The Tilton house illustrates the intense combination of influences that characterized McKim, Mead & White's designs of the early shingle style. In a single building one sees juxtapositions of details from Queen Anne, American colonial, Japanese, Islamic, and art nouveau designs as well as tantalizing images from the sketchbooks of Stanford White. The house suggests the best qualities of the firm in that same period, not in terms of any single artistic direction but for its evidence of collaboration, its demonstration of unbridled imagination, and its willingness to experiment. There is also a tentative quality to the completed design, not for what its architects failed to try but for what they failed to exclude. The three partners, who had been together for a little over a year, must have been on top of each other in their tiny office at 57 Broadway and might still have been trying to sort out the dynamics of the new partnership. Through its overwhelming generosity, the Tilton house suggests a temporary inability to select and develop a single main idea, a hesitancy that could have been rooted only in the powerful chemistry unleashed by the new partnership, held in check by the immense respect with which the partners regarded each other.

Intricate carving enhances all wooden surfaces. Clockwise from upper left: a bedroom mantelpiece; a panel in the entry hall; dining room sideboard; a transom panel in the music room.

Each of the bedrooms is finished with built-in cabinetwork and a handsome mantel. This inglenook recalls the entry hall downstairs and gives its chamber an added measure of privacy. Most of the wood throughout the house is pine finished in different colors.

The living room woodwork is painted a rich bottle-green with gold highlights. The combination of colonial and arts and crafts elements with proto-art nouveau motifs creates a intimate and dream-like interior.

# William Watts Sherman House

Newport, Rhode Island
Library alteration, 1881

N August 1881 McKim, Mead & White was invited to expand the library of the Watts Sherman house, which had originally been designed by Richardson in 1874. It is not clear why Sherman shifted his allegiance or why Richardson, whom one Chicago industrialist described as the "most dominating" personality he had ever met, allowed Sherman to stray. Richardson once said that he would "plan anything a man wants, from a cathedral to a chicken coop," but it is possible that an exercise in pure interior design fell outside even those generous limits. He may have directed Sherman to the young partnership because he was too busy himself, and he knew and respected at least two of the partners. Alternatively, Sherman may have contacted McKim, Mead & White directly when they were in Newport for the first full season of their celebrated Casino. Whatever the route by which it arrived, the commission gave White an opportunity to revisit the most important house design of his apprenticeship.

The entrance facade, acknowledged as the progenitor of the shingle style, is composed of bands of asymmetrical window groups and panels of textured cladding, all set underneath a generous gable and on top of a masonry base. The exposed library chimney provides a vertical counterpoint to the horizontal layering of the composition.

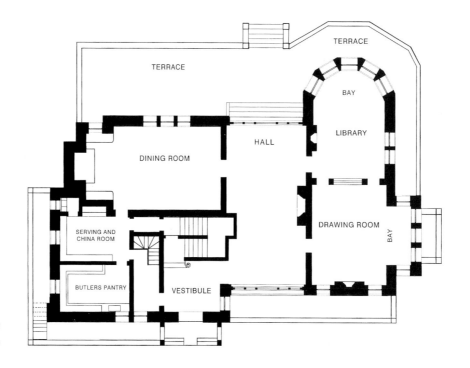

Ground floor plan of the original Richardson design. McKim, Mead & White joined the two rooms on the right by replacing two interconnecting doors with a large central pocket door.

Scalloped pediment above the door to the library. The waterlilies are an art nouveau motif.

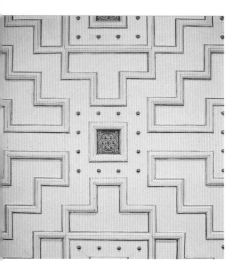

The ceiling features a pattern of interlocking rectangular geometry and regularly spaced ornamental accents.

Stanford White had worked for Gambrill & Richardson for six years, arriving in the spring of 1872 as a nineteen-year-old untrained painter and leaving in 1878 as Richardson's chief draftsman and principal assistant. Soon after White joined Richardson's office, McKim left to set up his own practice in the same building at 57 Broadway, recruiting William Rutherford Mead to assist him. Three months into White's tenure Richardson relocated to Brookline, Massachusetts; officially the office remained in New York until 1878. The Watts Sherman house was completed in the middle of White's career with Richardson. As the drawings were executed under White's supervision in New York, McKim and Mead must have looked at them and may even have lent a hand in their execution.

The Watts Sherman house is a landmark in the evolution of the shingle style. Under the shelter of its massive gables the house combines Richardson's easy flow of interior space with the formal vocabulary of the emerging Queen Anne revival style. It is unlike any American house that preceded it, and it had an immediate impact on late-nineteenth-century architecture. Later shingle style buildings by McKim, Mead & White and their contemporaries would retain its broad roof, horizontal groupings of windows, and rich surface textures, while replacing its overall "Englishness" with an American simplicity based on colonial prototypes.

How much of the original design is attributable to White cannot be established with certainty. Richardson must have determined the overall direction of the design, but he may have given White some freedom in its development; the details and lively textures of the exterior and interior are generally credited to him. Vincent Scully describes the project as "a close adaptation of Shaw's Queen Anne only under what might loosely be called the influence of Stanford White."

The 1881 commission called for enlarging the corner library to fill two adjoining suites. Realized with woodwork painted in a dense blue-green color, the new library is a foil to the dark wood finishes of the other living spaces, and it shows how far White had come since 1874. Its design illustrates the principal characteristics of the firm's early interiors, blending oriental exoticism with native iconography and contrasting near-boundless imagination with a strong underlying order. Gilded details accent geometric patterns on the ceiling and calligraphic flourishes on the casework, evoking images ranging from Japan and the Near East to Owen Jones and Tiffany. The scalloped niches flanking the fireplace expand the geography of allusions to include the American colonial tradition so esteemed by the three architects.

In about 1890, with Richardson in his grave and McKim, Mead & White at the height of their fame, Sherman changed architects again. His wife had died in 1884 and he had since married Sophia Brown of Providence. To accommodate her plans for a more active Newport social life, Dudley Newton converted half of the library into a ballroom and added a service wing to the north. His addition mimics the exteriors of the original house but muffles the impact of Richardson's monumental descending north gable. Considerably less sympathetic additions have been made over the past forty years. The house is currently used as a women's dormitory by Salve Regina University, which safeguards the library as a trustees' meeting room.

The rich interior vocabulary is composed of unusual combinations—scallop shells, Japanese motifs, panels and pilasters plus alternating patterns of meanders and fishscales—presented in a limited but dense palette of green and gold. The library's strict symmetry is relieved by bay at the left.

# Isaac Bell House

## Newport, Rhode Island
## 1881–83

ISAAC BELL'S VILLA is the perfect shingle style house. McKim, Mead & White's earlier designs chronicle the evolving dynamics of their young partnership as much as they illustrate the development of an architectural signature. Later country houses embody seeds of the neoclassical aesthetic that was to replace the shingle style's primitive vitality with a more academically correct language. But the Isaac Bell house is fully realized, inside and out, in its conception, its massing, and its details, as the complete expression of what Vincent Scully has called "the architecture of the American summer."

Isaac Bell was an appropriate patron for America's native style. The first Isaac Bell settled in Connecticut in 1640, and McKim, Mead & White's client was the thirteenth in a direct line of descendants to carry that name. Privately educated in New York, Bell started in banking and switched to his father's business as a cotton trader, moving to Savannah to be closer to the market. He had made his fortune and was retired by 1878 when, at the age of thirty-one, he married Jeannette Bennett, the younger sister of newspaper publisher James Gordon Bennett Jr. A year later Bennett would hire McKim, Mead & White to design the Newport Casino across the street from his Bellevue Avenue estate. The Bells must have been content to rent. By 1881 they had two children and were on their way to a third when they retained the firm to build on a corner lot two blocks south of the Casino. Their first full season in the house was 1883. Bell subsequently served as ambassador to The Netherlands during the Cleveland administration, and by the time of his death in January 1889, at the age of forty-two, he had spent only three summers in his own Newport cottage.

The design of the Bell house advances the synthesis of Queen Anne and modernized colonial influences that Richardson had initiated in the Watts Sherman house, but without the latter's "Englishness." Its exterior builds on the firm's earlier work, combining simplified volumes with richly textured surfaces and bold juxtapositions of forms. The elevations take up

Under the aegis of the Preservation Society of Newport County, the Bell house is undergoing a meticulous restoration that is expected to be completed in 1999. New shingles in Alaskan yellow pine will eventually weather to brown.

Extterior details include (left to right) a cartouche on the spandrel of the tower giving the date of completion of 1882; the projecting bay window of the master bedroom; an ornamented rainwater collector against the fish scale pattern shingles; one of a pair of dolphins supporting the porch roof over the front steps.

The inglenook in the entry
hall surrounds the tiled
fireplace with built-in
seating, leaded glass lights
and panels taken or copied
from French provincial
furniture. The unusually
wide spacing of the beaded
board imparts a monumental
scale to the walls.

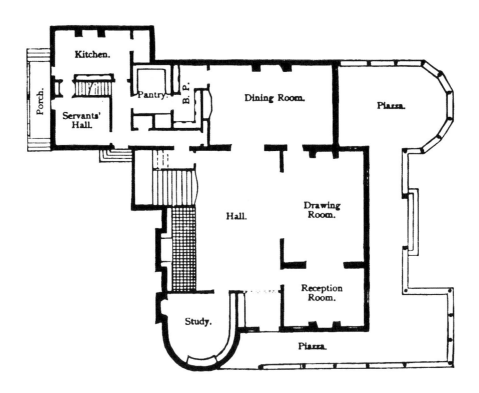

Ground floor plan.
The study was enlarged
about 1897.

where the south facade of the Samuel Tilton house left off: broad gables,
asymmetrical massing, horizontal bands of windows, and deep porches (which
the partners called piazzas), all set on a masonry base. Eaves and overhangs
are reduced to crisp shadow lines. Shingled walls are enriched by details
that derive as much from furniture design as from architecture, such as the
triple mock arched windows, the spindled corner bay, the dolphin porch
brackets, and the leaf-spring column capitals. The rubbed red brick and
pepperpot tower recall the Casino, but its textured balconies and screens
have been moved indoors and replaced on the facade with bands of shingles,
knife-edged shadow lines, and pure voids. While bamboo columns reflect
the vogue for Japonism that was always an undercurrent in the firm's early
work, most of the exterior details are pure Yankee.

The informal massing illustrates the shingle style's characteristic linkage
between exterior and interior volumes. The generous living hall at the heart
of the house becomes an armature supporting a collection of individual and
well-proportioned chambers. Major public rooms open onto this central core
through oversized doorways while the second floor is connected by the extra-
wide stairs, so that space flows effortlessly in a variety of directions. The plan's
pinwheel-like motion is initiated by its off-axis entrance and reinforced by
the cascade of daylight through major, off-center openings. This rotary movement eventually surfaces on the exterior in the push and pull of solids and
voids in the piazzas and towers projecting from the corners of the facade.

The hall contains one of the most interesting inglenooks in American architecture. Its fireplace is enclosed by wood screens, whose lattice-like transparency and textural density simultaneously separate and integrate the alcove into the adjacent staircase, reflecting and breaking up the light and giving the house a distinctly exotic flavor. Doweled wood screens in a variety of shapes, sizes, and functions were a principal component of the firm's design vocabulary from its earliest commissions. For Bell's front hall the architects abandoned any pretense at abstraction, cannibalizing whole panels from French provincial armoires and incorporating them into the walls of the house.

Other spaces are more chastely decorated only by comparison with the alcove. Oak planks cover the living hall, whose walls and ceiling are separated by a continuous frieze of colored, embossed wallpaper. The walls and ceiling of the adjoining dining room are finished with woven rattan, which is subdivided into panels by thin mahogany moldings. Polished brass escutcheons made from the perforated lids of bed warming pans are set into the walls above the wainscoting.

The dining room's built-in (but almost freestanding) neo-Georgian sideboard continues the tradition initiated in the Kingscote dining room, although its pierced metal overlays suggest an interest in more exotic ornamental sources. The reception room features a pale pastel palette of cream wallpaper, off-white trim with gold accents, and borders and tiles with matching tulip motifs, creating a tableau representative of the more bourgeois face of the aesthetic movement. Bedroom fireplaces are surrounded by colonial paneling, accented by the firm's characteristic spindled shelving. The master bedroom's corner bay evokes the romanticism of contemporary Gothic novels while its built-in cupboards recall McKim's interest in eighteenth-century Newport.

The most significant of these interiors are still intact. Bell's widow sold the house in 1891 to Samuel and Edna Barger, who had rented it in previous summers and who christened it Edna Villa. They expanded the library to its present dimensions around 1897. The Bargers and their descendants occupied the house until 1952; it was subsequently used as a year-round residence, a nursing home, and a law office. The Preservation Society of Newport County bought the house in 1994 and is restoring its architecture, decoration, and furnishings to the period of Isaac Bell's brief tenancy as a paradigm of the shingle style house.

Top: Detail of a door surround in the upstairs hall shows the convex reeding on the casing and a decorated corner block.

Above: The sideboard in the dining room illustrates the deliberate ambiguity between built-in and free-standing furniture.

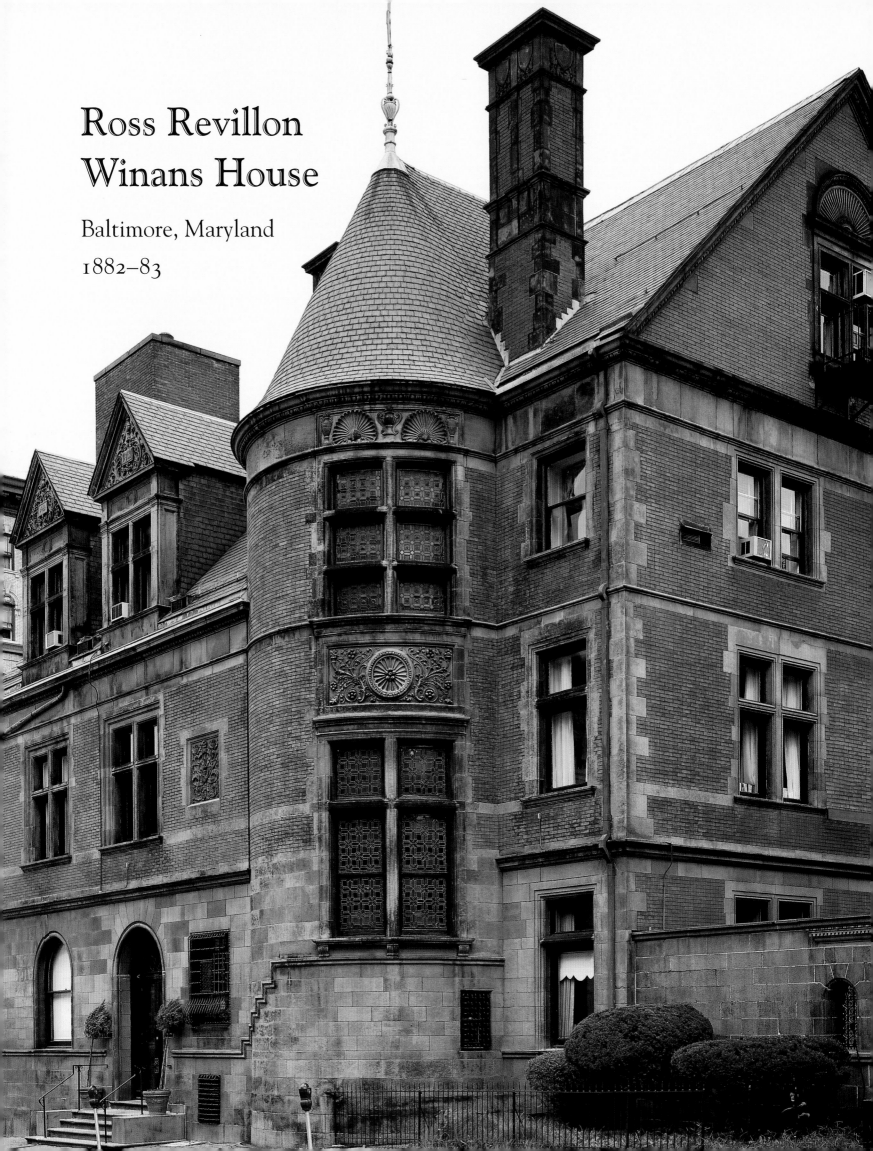

# Ross Revillon
# Winans House

### Baltimore, Maryland

### 1882–83

 Y THE MID-NINETEENTH CENTURY the Winans family was well established in Baltimore. Ross Revillon Winans's grandfather, for whom he was named, amassed a substantial fortune from his mechanical inventions for the Baltimore & Ohio and other railways. In 1843 he sent his sons, Thomas DeKay and William Louis Winans, to Russia to develop the rail link between St. Petersburg and Moscow; by 1850 they had contracted with the government to build and maintain the rolling stock and to establish shops along the route. Thomas Winans married Celeste Revillon, a Russian of French and Italian descent, in 1847 and their first child, Ross, was born in St. Petersburg in 1850. The family returned to the States a year later, taking up residence in a vast Baltimore mansion called Alexandrofsky and spending their summers in a Newport villa on Ocean Drive ironically, but appropriately, named Bleak House.

Ross Revillon Winans, who was said to have inherited twenty million dollars on his father's death, continued the house-building tradition. In 1882, three years after marrying his first cousin Neva Whistler, Winans hired McKim, Mead & White to design a new house in Baltimore, which

The Winans houses acknowledges McKim, Mead & White's debt to H. H. Richardson as well as an early interest in European prototypes for city houses. Urban sites and masonry construction suggested more formal plans and details than those of the shingled houses.

The entrance hall incorporates a rich collage of forms and textures, mostly realized in wood. The sensuous twist of the balusters contrasts with walls of endgrain blocks set flush in a tight lattice framework. The fireplace, the principal exception to the limited palette of color and materials, is realized in a brilliant blue glazed tile with mirror and brass fittings.

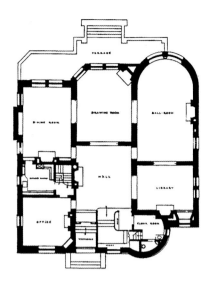

Ground floor plan.

was completed in 1883. White was the principal in charge of design; Cass Gilbert, a young architect in the firm, was the clerk-of-the-works.

Richardson himself could have sketched the plan of the Winans house from Brookline without ever going to Baltimore. The first floor is arranged as a pinwheel of rooms surrounding a living hall. The strong, simple forms of each space explode the confines of the square perimeter, creating offsets, pockets, and curves which, laid out as thick masonry walls, are translated into bays, arches, and towers. Richardson also could have specified the exterior materials, set the pitch of the main gable, and added the cone-shaped roof at the stair tower.

But the house is more than an exercise in second-guessing the Great Mogul, as White referred to his mentor. It is an original expression of the firm's interest in formal simplification as the starting point for the application of decoration. The roof is realized not as the rough-hewn overarching shelter and jagged ridge-line that Richardson favored, but as a polished plate, neatly creased and tightly folded over the sharp edges of the forms below. The texture of the individual stones is subordinated to the smooth, taut walls, allowing masonry to become a canvas for texture, color, and ornament. The irregular red brick box is firmly tied up with ribbons of flush limestone stringcourses. The vertical of rough blown glass set in leaded lights and enriched spandrels transforms the stair tower into a gigantic highboy, giving the term "street furniture" a new meaning. Croissets become beaded moldings, tympana at the dormers are clad in wavy copper shingles, chimneys are built of tiles set in a parquet pattern, and McKim's beloved colonial scallop shells appear in multiple locations. One direct reference to Richardson is the finial at the top of the stair tower, a tall roman candle burst of decorative metalwork that recalls White's rendering of the revised tower for Trinity Church.

Two commissions contemporary with the Winans house are the near-twin C. A. Whittier house in Boston and the triple town house for Charles L. Tiffany in New York. The similarity of the three structures in massing, material, and detail suggests that the young firm was developing a specific style for the urban villa, one that would appropriate a Richardsonian vocabulary of forms and materials and embellish their tightened surfaces with rich bursts of texture, color, and ornament. They abandoned this style almost as quickly as they had adopted it, moving on to other European models with flatter roofs, more symmetrical massing, and greater regularity in elevation.

The dimensions of individual rooms of the Winans house are generous, and the planning is remarkably flexible. The ground floor opens up

View through the living hall toward the front door, set at a level two steps below.

The doors and drawers of the sideboard in the dining room are sheathed with patinated and delicately pierced copper panels.

completely: the huge pocket doors are pushed back, allowing walls between the double hall, the ballroom and the dining room to disappear, and spatial divisions are apparent only in the individual decorative schemes. The dining room features a built-in sideboard presented as a piece of freestanding colonial furniture, but here finished with copper panels pierced with a pattern like Belgian lace. Other familiar colonial motifs such as the spindled staircase, paneled wainscoting, and turned legs are almost lost in the flood of imaginative details and rich materials. The stair hall is paneled in wood marquetry blocks, whose tight patterns of directional grain recall the back of an assembled jigsaw puzzle. Vivid blue tiles surrounding the fireplace in the entrance hall make it glow year-round with icy Turkish blaze. The walls of Winans's private study were originally finished in gesso duro, shot through with gold dust. His safe remains concealed behind a wood door hung on hammered brass hinges, with twin suns floating in a starlit field of bronze upholstery nails.

These rooms became the generous entertaining space Winans envisioned and they were often filled with guests. After 1907, when his wife and both their children died within a year, Winans became increasingly eccentric and reclusive. He lived alone in the house until his death in 1912. Since then the Winans house has been used as a school, a funeral home, and doctors' offices, and it is now owned by a preservation-minded publishing company.

Behind the massive door in Ross Winans's office was an equally large safe. The sunburst ornament is executed in upholstery tacks, while the walls were originally finished in decorative plaster mixed with gold dust.

The fireplace, sideboard and windows form a highly symmetrical composition in the dining room, with the door from the drawing room as the only off-center element.

Robert Goelet House

# Ochre Point

Newport, Rhode Island

1882–84

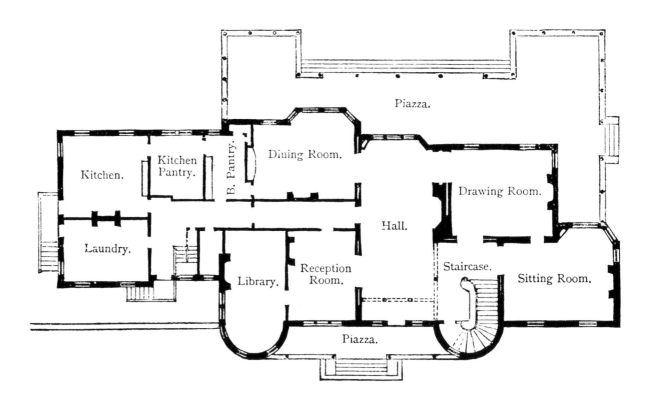

Ground floor plan. The geometry of the sea side is softened by multiple chamfers and setbacks, while the entrance side has more sharply defined edges and corners.

Piazza.

Kitchen.

Kitchen Pantry.

B. Pantry.

Dining Room.

Drawing Room.

Hall.

Laundry.

Library.

Reception Room.

Staircase.

Sitting Room.

Piazza.

OBERT GOELET HAD GOOD FORTUNE. He was born in 1841 into New York's Knickerbocker establishment, inheriting vast tracts of Manhattan real estate, managing his affairs with intelligence and discretion, and taking a long view of property ownership. Characterizing him as a private man with strong loyalties, Goelet's 1899 obituary calculated his major corporate directorships at five, his club memberships at twenty-nine, and his estate at twenty-five to forty million dollars.

Goelet also had good timing. Had he built a big Newport house prior to his marriage in 1879, he would probably have erected one of Richard Morris Hunt's half-timbered perpendicular villas. If he had waited until the end of the 1880s, his self-esteem as a member of America's hyper-moneyed class would have demanded an architecture with more explicit references to European nobility, preferably wrought in stone. Again Hunt might well have been his first choice. But for the five years following the 1880 completion of the Newport Casino, enlightened plutocrats ranging from the merely well-to-do to merchant princes like Robert Goelet wanted shingled cottages designed in the modern colonial style by McKim, Mead & White. Ochre Point, the grandest remaining shingle style house, was designed in 1882 and completed by 1884.

Ochre Point is a very big house, practically on the scale of an ocean liner, with at least seven levels, rooms beyond counting, and lots of summery elements including porches, dormers, bays, and lookouts. Its exterior displays all the details of the early shingle style, including sgraffito panels, cut shingles, skinny columns, knife-like eaves, broad roofs, and big chimneys with dovecote tops. The great shingled mass of the roof and upper stories meets the brick base at a sharply drawn datum line that circumscribes the entire building. The size and richness of the massing is offset by a relatively restrained palette of materials, consisting of cedar shingles, painted trim, and brick with bluestone details. The plain, broad frieze organizes the varied roofscape and identifies the family end of the house, duplicating the extent of the porches below. On the entrance side the front porch is framed by two rounded towers and surmounted by a pebbledash medallion. The off-center placement of the front door is consistent with the inherent informality of the building type and style. Landscaping is deliberately simple, consisting principally of a shallow earth berm that establishes a plinth for the house itself.

The spacious interior accommodates more public rooms than usual (dining and breakfast rooms, parlor and drawing room, library and billiard room) and just enough formal circulation to maintain order. The level of

The grandest of the shingle style houses, Ochre Point nonetheless uses a vocabulary of towers and porches, warm materials, animated patterns, and sheltering roofs to create a welcoming vision of summer leisure.

design, detail, and craftsmanship is consistently high throughout the house. Every room and every passage reveal architectural and decorative treats, but by any measure the main interior event is the supremely comfortable, two-story living hall, which organizes the plan and forms the heart of the house. It is an orgy of oak, ranging from polished, hand-hewn logs framing the ceiling to the cabinetmaker's perfection of the balcony, and it achieves the nobility of expression that Goelet sought in his summer house.

The building is substantially unchanged today. The breakfast room at the north end of the porch was enclosed after construction, as was an open sleeping porch located at the center of the third floor; a number of dormers have been added on both sides. In keeping with its high state of preservation, Ochre Point is one of the few remaining shingle style houses that retains its awnings.

At Ochre Point the decorative vocabulary of the early houses was raised to a level that tested the limits of the shingle style.

Decorated with bronze carpet nails and flanked by garlands of leaded glass, the front door opens into a shallow vestibule framing one end of the two-story hall.

Goelet and his architects referred to the Newport house as Southside, but Goelet's daughter-in-law eventually rechristened the family seat Ochre Point, observing that her property was not on the south side of anything in particular. The new name also paired Goelet's house more closely with Ochre Court, the 1891 limestone chateau that Hunt built across the street for Goelet's brother Ogden.

A built-in armoire and an heirloom desk flank arched bays at the vestibule. The frieze around the walls of the billiard room beyond is covered with embossed leather.

Combining monumentality with virtuosity and detail, Robert Goelet's house is a shingle style landmark, but it possesses an additional layer of cultural significance in its relationship to the two palaces on either side. Ochre Point demonstrates that the shingle style was essentially democratic, an American architecture applicable to residential programs of all sizes and for all levels of wealth. Ochre Point may be a European aristocrat in Jeffersonian dress, as suggested by the ambition of its decorative program, but it is size and not typology that differentiates the Goelet house from the more modest cottages the firm had been building elsewhere. By the mid 1880s the hyper-rich were beginning to demand architecture that celebrated the differences between them and their countrymen. Hunt's adaptation of the European model for the palaces of rich Americans would irreversibly

The living hall with its two-story paneled chimney breast is the heart of the house. A balcony surrounding the hall provides access to second floor bedrooms and to additional levels above.

Above: The fireplace wall in a guest bedroom includes the built-in cabinet work and colonial motifs found in the Tilton and Bell houses.

Opposite: The painted walls and woodwork of the drawing room contrast with the natural finishes and distinctly medieval fittings of the living hall and dining room beyond.

change the direction of McKim, Mead & White's residential practice. After the William G. Low house of 1886–87 the firm abandoned the shingle style, not because they had exhausted its potential for delight but because their clients no longer admired its egalitarian expression.

Robert Goelet remained loyal to his architects, whose style evolved to match his needs. Between 1885 and 1899 McKim, Mead & White built six commercial buildings and a mausoleum for the Goelet family. With fellow founder J. P. Morgan, Goelet commissioned the firm to design the new Metropolitan Club in 1891. The Goelet Cup, a nine-quart trophy for racing schooners, was designed by White in 1896, as was the frame for a portrait of Goelet's son. Goelet must have liked White's company as well, making the architect a gift in 1887 of membership in the Ristigouche River Salmon Fishing Club.

# The Villard Houses

New York

1881–85

n April 1881 Henry Villard purchased the land along the east side of Madison Avenue between Forty-ninth and Fiftieth streets, just across the street from St. Patrick's Cathedral, and commissioned McKim, Mead & White to build six houses on the site. Villard, a German immigrant, former reporter turned financier, and director of the Northern Pacific Railroad, planned to occupy the largest of these houses with his family and to sell the remaining five to business associates. Each buyer was expected to retain the firm to design the interiors. Catastrophic reversals forced Villard to abandon his residence before it was fully completed, and his architects were retained by only three of the other buyers to complete their far more modest shells. Nonetheless the Villard houses are important at every level. Together with the Newport Casino and the Boston Public Library, the Villard complex is one of the commissions that catapulted the office of McKim, Mead & White into the top echelon of American architects within a decade of its debut.

The partners were well known to Villard. His brother-in-law was married to McKim's sister, and in the previous year the Villards had retained McKim, Mead & White to enlarge their country house in Dobbs Ferry, a town on the Hudson just north of the city. Still, the commission to design an entire blockfront in a fashionable quarter was a remarkable coup for three young architects who had been in partnership for less than two years. Furthermore, Villard was determined to create a rival to the palaces that William Henry Vanderbilt and his two sons had recently completed on Fifth Avenue. Construction began in May 1882. In December 1883, with his business affairs rapidly disintegrating, Villard moved his family into their unfinished quarters, where they remained for less than six months before permanently relocating to Dobbs Ferry.

For the house group Villard and his architects followed the model of an Italian Renaissance palace, with individual rowhouse units subordinated to a single coherent block. Four of the six units are entered through a central

The fence enclosing the courtyard holds the street line along Madison Avenue and creates a princely entrance for four of the six houses.

The Villard houses were not the first example of a multiple-rowhouse ensemble, but they raised that building type to a level that has not been equaled in New York.

court, including Villard's own house, which filled the south end of the lot. The imposing arcade on the main courtyard facade actually leads to two separate houses, whose demising walls are located by the odd placement of quoining over the arcade.

The elevations are all but unique in their restraint, particularly in comparison with the prevailing taste for excess demonstrated in the neighboring residences of Villard's peers, and even in comparison with contemporary designs by the firm. The facades are based on generalized Italian Renaissance prototypes such as the Cancelleria, the Farnese Palace, and the Villa Farnesina, which the firm modified to reflect the specific attributes of Villard's site and program. The subtly different rustication of base, parlor floor, and quoining above are all relatively chaste, as are the plain profiled string courses marking various levels and the bracketed cornice capping the smooth four-story wall. The remaining ornament is limited to window surrounds on the three main floors, four stone balconies, and assorted medallions. The architects suggested that the block should be sheathed in white limestone as a tribute to its Renaissance antecedents and as a relief from

the ubiquitous brownstone of New York. At Villard's insistence the facades were executed in brownstone.

The Villard residence has always been the most important of the six. As originally finished by McKim, Mead & White, the public rooms in Villard's house took the firm's interiors to a level achieved in almost no other American residence up to that date. Stanford White supervised a team of fellow artists, including Augustus and Louis Saint-Gaudens, Maitland Armstrong, and possibly Tiffany or La Farge, plus legions of the city's leading artisans and craftsmen. They filled the lower floors with mantles, stained glass windows, mosaics, marquetry, and murals which in sheer quality and visual coherence easily surpassed the efforts of two generations of Vanderbilts up the street.

The walls of entry and living hall were clad in marble slabs, inlaid with flush, decoratively patterned panel strips and trimmed as classical mouldings. Mosaics in elaborate patterns covered the floors and vaulted ceilings. A novel clock, designed by Stanford White and decorated with signs of the zodiac by Augustus Saint-Gaudens, was set in the highly polished marble

After Whitelaw Reid took over Villard's residence from the bankrupt financier in 1886, Stanford White redecorated the two-story music room in white and gold. (Cervin Robinson)

The vestibule of Villard's unit illustrates both the vocabulary and the intensity of the firm's early decorative style. In Villard they had a client with the means and the will to surpass previous solutions. (Cervin Robinson)

walls of the great stair hall. An arcade and balustrade at the second floor was also realized in Siena marble and covered with high Renaissance chasing.

As they had from their earliest commissions, the designers assembled an entirely new decorative vocabulary with only a few borrowings from previous designs. Familiar details such as thick glass lenses in the leaded sidelights and nailheaded medallions on the doors appear episodically, but they are the exception. There is a music room, but unlike Tilton's music room in Newport, the walls of Villard's were enriched with bas relief panels of musical instruments and casts of Lucca della Robbia's Cantoria. A high wooden screen, city cousin to the one they designed for Kingscote, allowed the dining room to expand into the breakfast area. The dining room itself is finished in familiar oak, but its walls are enriched with marquetry frames and the frieze is decorated with quotations in five languages, inlaid in blond wood. Even the dimensions of the room are stylish, its long thin proportions emphasized by a shallow barrel vaulted ceiling enriched with plaster moldings and painted medallions. The effect is worthy of a Medici prince.

The collaboration did not end with Villard's departure. After the house was purchased from Villard's creditors by Whitelaw Reid and his wife, Elisabeth Mills Reid, in 1885, White and his team completed and redecorated the house, achieving the extent, arrangement, and appearance visible today. The Reids' most significant alterations were made to the drawing room. Originally, the walls and columns of the triple suite overlooking Madison Avenue were covered with an exotic densely figured marquetry of

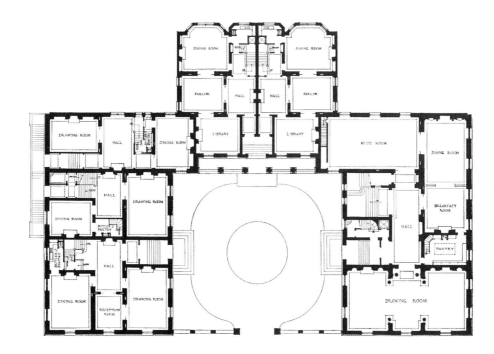

The plan from the firm's monograph was an idealized version of an interior layout that never existed. By the time the units at the left and center were finished (some by other architects), Whitelaw Reid had renovated Villard's house on the right

dark and light woods and mother-of-pearl. The contrast with the house's subdued exterior could not have been more striking, and the Reids must have agreed, for they immediately replaced the room with an open salon realized in pale green Callecotta marble under a gilded Renaissance ceiling. Villard's Renaissance-style marquetry was reinstalled in Ophir Hall, the Reids' medieval country house, which was also being renovated by McKim, Mead & White.

The design of the Villard block marks the beginning of McKim, Mead & White's commitment to the architecture of Bramante and Brunelleschi. In their use of Italian Renaissance prototypes, the firm employed a style that would eventually distinguish much of their urban work. Ironically, most scholars attribute the force behind this shift not so much to the original partners, but to the exceptional sophistication of their client Henry Villard, and the single-minded vision of their chief draftsman Joseph Morrill Wells. The partners' eventual embrace of the Italian Renaissance may have been inevitable, but it was Wells who forced them in that direction with their first monumentally ambitious commission.

The Villard houses, while private, also represent the firm's first significant public design in an urban setting and a breakthrough in the architectural ambitions and artistic standards of the period. A number of wealthy New Yorkers had built imposing townhouses with elaborate interiors before Villard. Some of these structures contained more than one household, some owners had assembled teams of professional artists, and one or two had even created distinguished interiors. The difference between those efforts and the Villard houses is quality, measured in the rigorous subordination of separate dwellings to the single block, the sublime restraint of the exterior elevations, and the unprecedented level and consistency of artistic achievement within.

Between 1885 and 1888 the firm finished three dwellings in the Villard complex for Edward Dean Adams and Harris C. Fahnestock. The two remaining neighbors, Artemas H. Holmes and Roswell Smith, retained others to complete their houses. All units remained privately owned and somewhat lightly occupied through World War II. In 1946 the north half of the complex was purchased by Random House as their headquarters. In 1948 the Archdiocese of New York acquired the southern half, including the Villard/ Reid house, turning its magnificent rooms into equally splendid chancery offices. In 1978 the western portion was replaced by a high-rise hotel and the remaining houses were converted into a variety of public and semi-public uses. Today the Villard/Reid house is the setting for an elaborately decorated restaurant, and its landmark interiors are temporarily obscured.

The upper stair hall of Villard's house reflects the materials, design, and tone of the whole interior. (Cervin Robinson)

# Montauk Point Association Houses

## Montauk, Long Island

## 1882–83

HE HOUSES BUILT IN 1883 for the Montauk Point Association are among the freshest of the firm's designs. Once preserved by neglect and a benign assortment of inappropriate uses, they have now been restored as private houses. Their continued occupancy demonstrates the contemporary nature of their original program and suggests that late-nineteenth-century settings created for the recreation of the professional class are perfectly appropriate for ordinary life at the end of the twentieth.

In 1879 Arthur Benson, fishing enthusiast and shipping magnate (and developer of Bensonhurst, Queens), bought the eastern tip of Long Island's south fork from the local farmers for one hundred fifty-one thousand dollars. Envisioning an elite summer colony devoted to outdoor pursuits and a relatively informal social life, he assembled the Montauk Point Association. His partners in the enterprise were a group of like-minded New York businessmen including merchant and financier Alexander E. Orr, lawyers Robert and Henry de Forest, author and Grolier Club founder William Loring Andrews, businessman Henry Sanger, banker Alfred Hoyt, and ophthalmologist and public-health pioneer Dr. Cornelius Agnew.

They consulted Frederick Law Olmsted to plan a community of vacation lodges and limited common facilities overlooking the Atlantic Ocean. The landscape plan distributed the home sites in a meandering line along the contours of a ridge, giving all houses a water view and endowing the collective development with an attractively informal air. A clubhouse was located in the middle, with a laundry and stable set at the rear of the compound. The plan minimized visible interventions, connecting all structures with a network of unpaved paths. The land surrounding the houses was originally open moor and pasture. Changes in the mild, humid microclimate, in combination with the elimination of farming, have allowed the subsequent growth of a dense concealing underbrush, from which only the peaks of the roofs are now visible.

For a group of busy and enlightened New York professionals looking

Entrance to the de Forest house. The open rosette from the interior of the Newport houses is used here as an exterior element.

The generous porches of the Association houses overlook the Atlantic Ocean at the easternmost tip of Long Island.

TOPOGRAPHICAL
MAP OF
THE GROUNDS
OF THE
MONTAUK
ASSOCIATION.
SUFFOLK COUNTY—
~ LONG ISLAND
N.Y.

LAKE
WYANDANCH

*Description of the Property.*

EXPLANATORY

ATLANTIC OCEAN

The map indicates the
clubhouse (5) and the
houses: Agnew (1),
Benson (2), Sanger (3),
Hoyt (4), Andrews (6),
de Forest (7), and Orr (8).
The photograph taken
in the mid 1880s shows
the arrangement of the
houses along the ridge
and the open fields sur-
rounding them. (Courtesy
Carlton Kelsey)

for an architect to design a modern resort community in the spring of 1882,
McKim, Mead & White was a logical choice. Richard Morris Hunt may have
been the most famous architect in America at that time, but after 1879 his
practice was directed more toward millionaires' palaces than rustic retreats.
Richardson was solidly ensconced in Boston. His protégés McKim, Mead &
White were in New York and, having recently completed the Newport
Casino for New Yorker James Gordon Bennett Jr. and Clayton Lodge in
upstate Richmond Springs for the ailing Cyrus McCormick, their creden-
tials as designers in a modern informal style were well established. With
commissions including Henry Villard's Madison Avenue town-house block
and Robert Goelet's Newport villa in hand by February, they must have
been the architects of the moment.

Between March and July seven of the eight members of the Association
retained the firm to design houses ranging from four thousand (Benson) to
seven thousand (Hoyt) square feet, while the Association itself (through

The Benson house, with
its slightly pagoda-like
aspect, recalls the period's
fascination with the Orient.
The original entrance
may have been around the
corner to the right, facing
the clubhouse. One of
the eyebrow windows is
a recent addition.

Henry G. de Forest, treasurer) commissioned the clubhouse and support buildings. The houses consisted of porches, living rooms, dining rooms, lots of bedrooms, and limited kitchen, pantry, and bathroom facilities. A simple life was not a servantless one. Some of the houses had back stairs, and the Hoyt house had a servants' dining room, separated from the kitchen by a breezeway. The entrance to each house faced toward the two-story clubhouse, which featured a large dining room downstairs and guest rooms above. All structures were built by Mead & Howells of Cornwall-on-Hudson, the firm's favorite contractor for Long Island work. Materials were shipped to the site by train, boat, and then wagon, a logistical consideration that must have encouraged the use of simple finishes and interchangeable parts.

The seven houses are individually distinct but united by similarities in size, scale, and massing, by their generous porches, and by common exterior cladding. All houses feature shingled roofs and upper stories, set in most cases over a painted clapboard base, a shingle style adaptation of the

Ocean facade of the de Forest house. This elevation shows the full array of textures and details that constituted the exterior vocabulary of the shingle style.

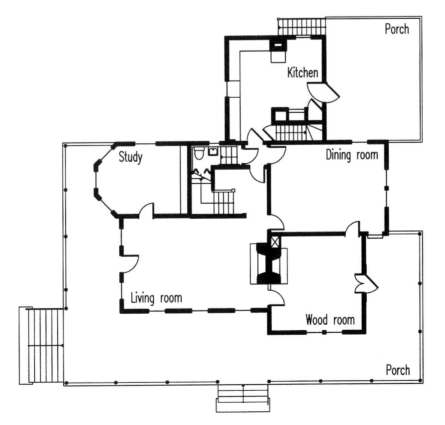

Contemporary drawings for the reconstruction of the Orr house, which was destroyed by fire in March 1997. Most of the drawings for small houses from this period were lost when McKim, Mead & White moved from 57 Broadway to 1 West 20th Street in 1891. (Courtesy James Hadley, AIA, WASA)

The Andrews house. A
system of interlocking and
repeating gables makes this
house simultaneously simple
and complex. Doweled
screens distinguish the main
entrance from the back
door and give a measure
of privacy to the master
bedroom porch, which
looks out to the ocean.

The Sanger house. Near-flush detailing at the eaves enhances the contrast of solid and void. The hip roofs at the dormers were part of a deliberate effort to subordinate the long side elevation to the main gable, which faced the clubhouse. The original entrance was through the end of the angled porch.

prototypical Queen Anne masonry plinth. The shingles are presented in a variety of contrasting shapes, patterns, and textures to emphasize gables, animate string courses, or decorate blank walls. The clubhouse was encircled by a waist-high band of diamond-cut units, set in contrast to the smooth geometries of wall, bay, porch, and roof.

The massing is based on major gables enriched by minor accents—dormers, turrets, eyebrows, upstairs porches—whose varied appearance and asymmetrical arrangement coincides with the apparently casual distribution of the houses along the ridge and reinforces the informal image of the compound. Most individual elements recall colonial or vernacular precedents; the broad, shallow roof of the Benson house hints at a fashionable interest in Japan.

Development of the exterior details is anything but casual. Trim is held flush to the wall and intersections of roof and wall planes are crisply detailed. Windows and doors, designed and located to satisfy internal requirements and to capture prevailing breezes, are ganged in sets, with decorative blind panels filling in the blank spaces. Casings are limited to beaded and flat moldings; porches have no soffits; and columns, spindles, and screens are made up of sticks turned on a lathe. This is architecture at its leanest and richest.

The interiors combine rustic simplicity with sophisticated planning and bursts of imagination. The house plans fall into two types, one a variation of the traditional colonial center hall with its staircase parallel to one wall and the other an extension of the Richardsonian living hall with large unfolding staircase and no formal circulation connecting public rooms. The

Above, left: A bedroom in the Hoyt house where the paneling of the fireplace surround is extended onto the ceiling.

Above, right: The master bedroom in the Andrews house, with the view from the porch to the ocean.

Opposite: A sitting room in the de Forest house has the same restrained decorative treatment: the focal point of the room is the fireplace executed in flat pine panels with pairs of jig-cut brackets supporting the mantel.

interior finishes consist principally of beaded board walls and ceilings, reeded trim, simple wood panels, and occasional plaster. Wood plank ceilings in the generous living halls are decorated with strips of lath. The banister in the de Forest house evokes Islamic geometries, while wooden screens in the Sanger and Hoyt stair halls recall more lessons from Japanese architecture.

The clubhouse burned down in 1933. The Orr house, destroyed by fire in 1997, has been reconstructed. Five of the other six houses are substantially intact, although most have been changed to one degree or another since they were first built. Porches have been rearranged, doors and windows moved, and kitchens, bathrooms, laundries, heating systems, and similar modern conveniences have been added. It is unlikely that periodic reshingling has preserved all of the original patterns and textures. Nonetheless, the houses retain their free-spirited robustness and would easily be recognized by their designers today.

Above: Pantry in the Hoyt house (left) and the living hall in the Sanger house.

Above, right: Living hall in the Sanger house. This room was the principal entrance and circulation space in the house.

Opposite: The staircase in the Sanger house uses the same vocabulary as the Tilton house—a large window on the landing, a built-in bench, and a continuous horizontal screen—but the execution is much simpler.

# John Forrester Andrew House

Boston

1883–86

OHN FORRESTER ANDREW was a career public servant, representing Back Bay and Beacon Hill in state and national offices from 1880 to 1893. A champion of civil-service reform, he established a reputation for political independence. In mid-career he ran for governor of Massachusetts and was narrowly defeated in his attempt to capture the office once held by his father, Governor John A. Andrew, whose Civil War efforts included fielding the legendary black 54th Regiment under Colonel Robert Gould Shaw.

The younger Andrew was four years behind McKim at Harvard and may have known the architect through their families' abolitionist connections. In July 1883, shortly before his marriage to Harriet Thayer, he retained McKim, Mead & White to design a house in newly fashionable Back Bay, the first of twenty Boston commissions the firm would ultimately receive. Nathaniel Thayer, his fiancée's father, had been one of the principal developers of the area, and the Andrew site at the corner

Plans of the first, second and third floors. Andrew's library and office on the first floor allowed him to receive official visitors at home.

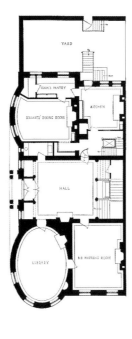

of Hereford Street and Commonwealth Avenue may have been one of the six corner lots he retained.

The development of Boston's Back Bay began in 1856. The former tidal flats were reclaimed, filled with gravel, and subdivided into lots, allowing for the construction of the Public Garden at the east end and the creation of Boston's grand boulevard, Commonwealth Avenue, linking the capital to its western suburbs. In contrast to the meandering pre-colonial patterns of Beacon Hill, Back Bay was laid out on a grid. Its blocks were filled with bow-fronted rowhouses occupied by middle- and upper-middle-class families. Building lots along the north side of Commonwealth Avenue commanded higher prices because they allowed the winter sun to fill the rooms at the front of each house, while corner lots guaranteed direct light to all rooms.

Managing to be both contextual and distinctive, the Andrew house raises the standard of Back Bay's vernacular architecture. An elliptical tower transforms the ubiquitous bow-front into a device for celebrating the corner of the block. Thick, undulating walls topped by a cornice and balustrade of equal gravity acknowledge Boston's Georgian heritage and evoke subliminal memories of London terraces, Florentine palaces, and Roman monuments. The decorative potential of each surface, material, and component is explored and exploited, while the overall composition maintains an air of cultivated restraint.

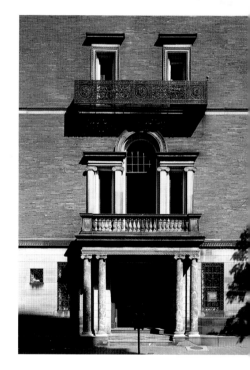

Above the entrance porch an elegant balcony and a Palladian window with floor-to-ceiling sash mark the living hall on the second floor. The wrought iron railing is said to have come from Versailles.

The distinction between semi-public space and family quarters was reinforced by the cool finishes of the downstairs hall and the columned screen, which flanks a throne-like seat at the foot of the staircase.

The elevations reveal their pedigree in the details. The twin bays on Hereford Street bracket a ducal porch, which is supported by columns of St. Laurent marble and topped by a majestic Palladian window. A band of endless knots separates the lightly rusticated stone base from the smooth upper walls of umber speckled brick. Double-hung sashes with single panes, iron balconies from the Palace of the Tuileries, and limestone balustrades and stringcourses all cleave to the undulating plane of the street wall, which is punctuated in stately rhythms by punched openings and classical surrounds.

The facade's ordered dignity, subdued tonal range, and emphasis on the horizontal continuity of the street wall all suggest a mild reprimand to the picturesque individuality of its earlier neo-Tudor neighbors. Only a decade had passed since the apogee of Ruskin's influence on American architecture, but the selection and arrangement of exterior forms, colors, and materials in the Andrew house continue the growing revival of Renaissance imagery and the emergence of the City Beautiful movement. McKim, Mead & White's Public Library of 1887–95 is the firm's major contribution to Boston's Beaux-Arts architecture, but the city was transformed as much by Olmsted's romantic landscapes as by the work of its classically inspired architects.

Inside the Andrew house the emerging classical sensibility of the exterior is present only in embryonic form. Four stories of public and private rooms illustrate the young firm's enthusiastic approach to prevailing haute bourgeois taste for rich finishes. The delicacy of the Italian mantle and the white marble mosaic floor of the entry are quickly forgotten among the dark wood, elaborate moldings, and leather-trimmed walls of the main hall, dining room, and stairway above. As if to demarcate the limits of male and female preserves, the drawing room and library overlooking Commonwealth Avenue are realized in lighter woods and more academically correct orders, enlivened with gilded trim, complex marquetry, enframed tapestries, allegorical ceilings, and colored marbles. The front rooms reveal the period's emerging cosmopolitan aesthetic and suggest what was hidden by the deep shadows in contemporary portraits of upper-crust Bostonians, such as Sargent's *The Children of Edward D. Boit*.

Each space or element is enhanced with nuances that reveal the designers' eclectic interests as well as their personal connections to contemporary artists and their own powerful imaginations. The living hall features a vigorous and naive classicism recalling Elizabethan paneling, while the fluted oak columns standing on strapwork pedestals are decorated with graceful twisting vines, a motif that appears simultaneously in the reliefs of Saint-Gaudens, the paintings of Dewing, and windows of La Farge. As with

On the second floor the polished wood of the stair flows into a richly paneled living hall. The foliate columns connect the decorative scheme to the art of the American Renaissance. The balance of the woodwork recalls early English Renaissance prototypes.

earlier houses, furniture becomes architectural and vice versa. The ingle-nook at the bottom of the stairs is presented as a throne, while the panel-ing in the upper hall grows into benches lining the walls. Bedrooms on the upper stories feature built-in dressers made of exotic hardwoods and operated with elaborate hardware, transforming domestic necessities into illustrations of the complexity, organization, and self-confidence of the Victorian household.

Both the architects and the clients were satisfied with the results. No sooner was his residence completed than Andrew commissioned the club-house for the Algonquin Club a block away on Commonwealth Avenue. Ten years later, McKim, Mead & White replicated the exterior of the Andrew house in their residence for Prescott Hall Butler at the corner of Park Avenue and Thirty-Fifth Street in New York.

John Forrester Andrew continued to live at 32 Hereford Street until his death in 1895. His daughter Cornelia Andrew Clark inherited the house, and her family lived there until 1950 when they sold the building to its current owners, the MIT chapter of Phi Chi Fraternity.

## LeRoy King House

# Berkeley House

## Newport, Rhode Island
## 1884–86

 F ALL THE CHANGES TO Berkeley House since McKim, Mead & White began the project early in 1884, the most significant intervention occurred before construction was underway. Drawings submitted to contractors for bids that spring indicate the granite stair tower and pebbledash gables, but they also show the walls clad in wood shingles with the firm's standard array of textural devices. The impetus for the last-minute change to brick must be attributed to the owner, LeRoy King.

The Kings were old Newport. LeRoy's father, Edward King, had made a fortune in the China trade and was the largest landowner in town. In 1845 he commissioned Richard Upjohn to design a three-story red brick Italian villa overlooking the harbor. One of Edward's brothers, William Henry, had bought Upjohn's neo-Gothic confection next door and renamed it Kingscote. Another brother, Dr. David King Sr., was the first president of the Newport Historical Society.

The Kings became loyal clients of McKim, Mead & White. In 1880 David King Jr. hired the firm to expand Kingscote, which he was renting from his uncle. Three years later LeRoy's widowed mother, Mary LeRoy

The original construction drawings of the elevations specified shingles on the walls, stone at the stair tower, and pebbledash in the gables and over the entrance porch. (Private collection)

King, commissioned her second McKim, Mead & White town house on Fifth Avenue. Between 1887 and 1906 LeRoy's brother George Gordon King II retained the firm to build and twice to expand a huge shingled Newport cottage called Edgehill on Harrison Avenue near Beacon Rock.

LeRoy King was raised in Newport and New York and educated at St. Paul's School and Columbia College. In 1881 he married Ethel Rhinelander, whose Knickerbocker family still owned major tracts of land throughout Manhattan. The site for their Newport villa was at the foot of Bellevue Avenue, across the street from Kingscote and the Isaac Bell house. The couple had been spending summers in a cottage on the property and were in no apparent hurry to build. King held the completed drawings for almost a full year before construction of his new house began in brick.

One pebbledash gable remains, overlooking the street entrance.

LeRoy King may have changed the material to match more closely his father's villa two blocks away. Alternatively, he may have sensed that shingles were no longer the right material for Bellevue Avenue. In any case, the house as built comes as a surprise. Only when pebbledash is substituted for the red slate gables on the garden facade and the walls below are imagined in variegated patterns of cut shingles set in crisply detailed planes does Berkeley House relate to McKim, Mead & White's previous Newport designs. The house makes more sense as an early example of the firm's brief transitional period, representing its shift from native precedents to the European roots of the Queen Anne style. The articulated forms, warm tones, and fanciful combinations of masonry in the King house indicate that McKim, Mead & White were examining contemporary revivals of European styles in their search for the proper expression of a gentleman's house.

While the architects were looking abroad for inspiration on the elevations, they began to rely more heavily on traditional eighteenth-century

colonial models for the rooms within. The interiors of the Berkeley House are characterized by a sober presentation of such Georgian motifs as raised paneling and recessed china cupboards in the dining room, twisted newels and balusters on the staircase, and Palladian windows at the landing and dormers. This conservative vocabulary announces the eventual rejection, by the architects and by their clients, of the exoticism of the firm's early interiors.

King's subsequent improvements to his property respond to the approach of the twentieth century. The careful organization of his household bills suggests an orderly personality, and the wide range of services they cover illustrates the contradictory details of a civilization straddling two irreconcilable periods. In 1887 King was running steady accounts with his

horseshoer and carriage trimmer, but by 1890 he was renting a telephone from the Providence Telephone Company. In 1893 Scannevin & Potter, Electrical Engineers & Contractors, proposed to wire the new house and original cottage with metered service, fuseboxes, and fifty-six outlets. Two years later Henry W. Cozzens repaired the front doorbell, sending King a bill on letterhead that promoted the installation of burglar alarms.

LeRoy King died in 1895, leaving three young children, LeRoy, Frederic, and Ethel. The younger LeRoy would later be a Harvard classmate and close friend of Larry White, Stanford White's only child; LeRoy and Larry dined with White on June 25, 1906, the night he was killed. Frederic King became an architect. The alterations that he implemented at Berkeley

The fireplace wall in the dining room recalls similar designs in the eighteenth-century quarter of Newport.

The open planning of shingle style houses connects the living hall to all public rooms while the beamed ceiling emphasizes the horizontal flow of space. The woodwork was originally unpainted.

House chronicle the growth of Newport as well as the evolving needs and tastes of the King family. He erected the brick wall to screen out the noisy and invasive procession up and down Bellevue Avenue and added the east wing, consisting principally of servants' rooms. At the same time he replaced the original earth plinth around the house with a paved terrace, expanded the library with a bay window, and replaced the pebbledash in the south gables with red slate. He was unable to dissuade his sister, Ethel, from painting over the natural wood interiors. Various members of the King family continued to own Berkeley House until 1985, and the structure remains in private hands.

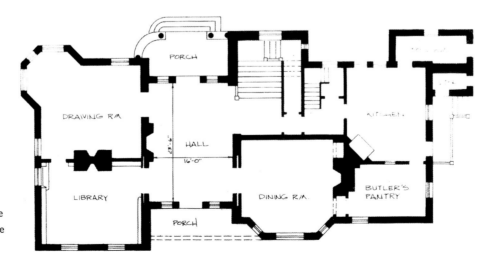

Ground floor plan. The angled projection of the living room bay was an urban gesture marking the corner of Bellevue Avenue and Berkeley Street.

Joseph Hodges Choate House

# Naumkeag

Stockbridge, Massachusetts

1885–86

JOSEPH HODGES CHOATE was a legendary figure in the world of law, politics, and diplomacy. In the course of a sixty-two-year professional career, he convinced the Supreme Court to find the income tax unconstitutional, organized the fall of Boss Tweed and his Tammany Ring, founded the New York Bar Association, served as president of the New York State Constitutional Convention, represented the United States at the 1907 Hague Conference of the Universal Peace Congress, and spent six years in London as the American ambassador to the Court of St. James. He made a fortune in the law, representing large corporations such as Bell Telephone and litigating the wills of William H. Vanderbilt,

In this view of the porte cochere and front door the house could easily be mistaken for a cottage by Shaw or Lutyens. The compass rose set in the pavement is a particularly English touch.

A. T. Stewart, and Samuel J. Tilden. According to his daughter Mabel, he was "brought up on the traditions of English law and history, and steeped in English literature." His anglophilia found some measure of expression at Naumkeag, his country house in Stockbridge, Massachusetts.

Stockbridge and neighboring Lenox were major Berkshire resorts. They offered a longer and less-structured season than Newport, as well as an impressive list of summer residents drawn from the aristocratic and professional classes of Boston and New York. Lenox was known for its stock of marble "cottages," including at least one copy of the Petit Trianon, and Shadowbrook, then the largest house ever built in the United States, which was destroyed by fire in 1956. Stockbridge may have been more modest architecturally, but by 1887 it did feature a casino and an attractive granite

On the entrance facade the dormers are subordinated to the thatch-like roof with the help of soft rounded corners and a near-total absence of trim. The Norman towers are straight out of White's European sketchbooks.

On the garden elevation the familiar shingle style vocabulary of tightly disciplined planes and staccato textures has been given a more sculptural quality.

Opposite: The stair hall illustrates the sobriety of the transitional interiors. Naumkeag is one of the few houses of this period in which the woodwork was not subsequently painted.

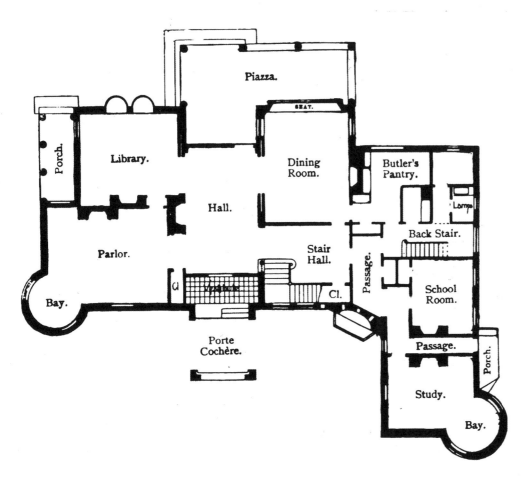

Ground floor plan. The simple four-square colonial plan has been massaged to create an entrance court with a sculpture niche in the main angle of the house and picturesque corner towers from Normandy.

The extension of the open stairway to the third floor replicates the vertiginous slope of the hill outside and connects the living hall to the family quarters on all levels.

Episcopal church, in addition to Choate's house, all designed by McKim, Mead & White.

Encouraged by two of his law partners to join them in Stockbridge, Choate persuaded his opponent in the Boss Tweed case to sell him forty acres on Prospect Hill, looking out to Monument Mountain. In 1885 Choate began to create a country seat with the advice of his friend McKim. The architect was just finishing two projects in the area, a house in Lenox for his fiancée, Julia Appleton, and St. Paul's Church in Stockbridge for Choate's partner Charles E. Butler, father of his friend and early client Prescott Hall Butler. Having rejected Olmsted's suggestion of siting the house halfway up the hillside, Choate retained another landscape designer, Nathan F. Barrett, who established the present location of the house at the high end of the property. The busy McKim recommended Stanford White as partner in charge of its design, a suggestion that Choate must have accepted gracefully. He remained one of McKim's most loyal supporters and was instrumental in the firm's selection as architects for Harvard University.

Original furniture and fittings preserve the welcome of the living hall. The ship's lantern and the hood over fireplace suggest that Choate was not averse to unusual juxtapositions.

The house was completed late in 1886, and the Choates moved
in the next spring. It was not until 1896 that the family called it Naumkeag
or "Haven of Peace," the Indian name of Choate's birthplace, Salem, Massachusetts.

The house has two distinct personalities; one elevation is rendered in
masonry, the other in wood. The brick entrance facade recalls White's
European sketchbooks, colored by images of rural England. Its picturesque
asymmetry is built up of bell-shaped towers, dormers softly wrapped in
roofing shingles, and a porte cochere whose quaintly hobbled ridge line and
rounded peak are still visible underneath the ivy. Massive and irregularly
placed chimneys punctuate the roofline without suggesting a rigorous internal order. The decorative potential of materials is evident in the rubble stone
walls, diaper patterns in the brick tower, millstone paving at the entry, and
shards of glass embedded in mortar joints.

The nascent monumentality, sharp geometry, and crisp details of the
firm's early designs are wholly absent from the entrance facade and only
faintly suggested at the rear elevation. Wall planes are more sculptural than

The dark paneling and arts
and crafts style furniture of
the library contrasts with
the more formal drawing
room, which was decorated
in a European style. The
Chinese Export porcelain
in both rooms was part of
Mabel Choate's collection.

architectural, with undulations to accommodate porches, bays, offsets, and concave shingled eaves. The twin cross gables recall the LeRoy King house, which is Naumkeag's exact contemporary and a similar case of experimentation in choice of materials, but the Stockbridge house is significantly softer in its realization than any Newport sibling.

The interior layout reflects the house's steep, difficult site. Space is organized around the great vertical gesture of the staircase, an apotheosis of varnished carved oak that connects all three main floors. Individual room sizes are modest, and space flows across the center hall without opening up the plan to any significant degree. The first floor may have been based on the model of a four-square colonial house, but irregularities and accommodations nudge the planning away from Cartesian order and toward picturesque asymmetry. The result is a house of immense charm, designed for family living rather than large-scale entertaining.

Choate's daughter Mabel lived in the house until her death in 1958. The interiors are virtually unchanged. The furniture, finishes, and fittings represent the conservative end of the arts and crafts taste in contrast to the decorative exuberance of the firm's earlier designs. Significant exceptions include the great carved chimney hood in the hall, the tin foil ceiling in the dining room, and decorative inspirations such as the beaded necklace carved into the library mantel.

The present landscape design with its sequence of exterior "rooms" is the result of Mabel Choate's thirty-year collaboration with Fletcher Steele, a Boston landscape architect. Miss Choate bequeathed Naumkeag to The Trustees of Reservations, who operate it as a house museum.

China and glassware were stored in the pantry adjoining the dining room. A knife cleaner sits on a shelf under the servants' call box; to the left is the dumbwaiter on which food was brought up from the kitchen below.

Detailing in the library includes a carved string of beads; Joseph Choate's study (far right) was decorated with Morris-inspired wallpaper and a federal style mantel.

Stanford White House

# Box Hill

St. James, Long Island  1885–1902

The triple gable entrance facade (preceding pages) is the result of two expansions of the original farmhouse (opposite). The multiple overlapping gables on the rear facade (below) suggest a greater degree of complexity. After the last expansion White covered the original clapboard exteriors with pebbledash, a mixture of beach pebbles embedded in wet cement.

TANFORD WHITE created Box Hill as a country seat for his family, which by 1887 consisted of his wife, Bessie Springs Smith, his son, Lawrence Grant White, and his widowed mother, Alexina Mease White. Sited on a hill overlooking St. James Harbor, Box Hill was surrounded by the farms and homesteads of his wife's relatives. The immediate neighbors included Bessie's three sisters, Cornelia Butler, Kate Wetherill, and Ella Emmett, for each of whom White or McKim designed or expanded houses with similar harbor views. Bessie's sense of family kept her in St. James more often than her husband, and White expected that his country house would always be filled with children. After his death in 1906 the Whites—widow, son, and mother-in-law—continued to live in Box Hill, and the house has been owned successively by White's son, who raised his eight children there, his grandson F. L. Peter White, who raised eleven, and his

Ground floor plan. Even after three major expansions the front door of the farmhouse remains in its original location. (Courtesy Buttrick White & Burtis Architects)

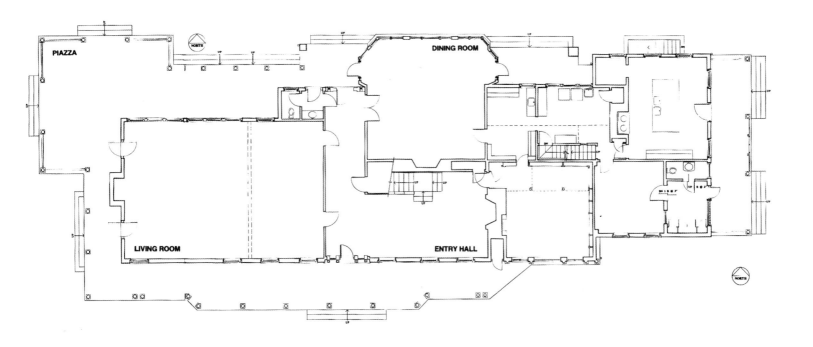

The landscape combined large open stretches with steps, parterres, and formal gardens. Photographs from the turn of the century show the view from the rear terrace toward Long Island Sound (above) and from the front porch (below). (Private collection)

Today the water view is obscured, but the serenity of the landscape remains intact.

great-grandson Daniel W. White. Box Hill is one of two McKim, Mead & White houses still occupied by the families for whom they were built.

Stanford White maintained significant households in the city and in the country. He believed that an architect must live better than his clients, and he developed both his Gramercy Park town house and Box Hill as expressions of that ideal. But he would have to achieve that effect economically. With the expansion of the office during the 1880s, White may have been relatively prosperous, but unlike his clients he had no personal fortune. While the Gramercy Park residence was furnished (one might say crammed) with portable treasures obtained through his European dealers, the building itself was rented. Thanks to his wife's inheritance, Box Hill represented an opportunity to achieve a similar degree of grandeur, but still within constraints.

Over the next twenty years, and with McKim and Mead's encouragement and advice, White tinkered with, redesigned, and enlarged the original 1850s farmhouse into a 15,000 square foot manor house on seventy-eight acres with a full complement of barns, cottages, support facilities, and landscape improvements. Box Hill combines visual elements that both recall and anticipate the full span of White's career, from the doorknobs of the Tilton

The unusual combination of materials—golden split bamboo on the walls and terra-cotta tiles on the floor—gives the stair hall an exceptional warmth. The limestone mantel, supported by grotesque satyrs, is surmounted by a painted and gilded panel from an Italian chest.

The saw-toothed profile and green glazed tile give the stair a monumental character. The lions are carved in wood with gilded accents.

house to the mantels of Rosecliff. With a regular cadre of weekend guests it became a center of his social life and a laboratory for his architectural ideas.

The landscape of Box Hill celebrates the pastoral sweep of Long Island's North Shore with a collage of artifacts from different times and cultures, illustrating the eclecticism for which the firm in general, and White in particular, became known. Rhododendron allées, white graveled driveways, shingled carriage barns and water towers, broad lawns, formal gardens, and even a Greek revival orangerie appeared in a sequence between the main gates and the house. Crisp plantings and modern conveniences—White was intensely interested in the automobile—were juxtaposed against arcadiana—temples, pergolas, herms, and sarcophagi, while new construction was combined with older artifacts. Bluestone steps were salvaged from the Croton Reservoir at Fifth Avenue and Forty-second Street, and white marble paving from the A. T. Stewart mansion at Thirty-fourth Street and Fifth Avenue.

The expansion of the house from cottage to country seat required four major building programs, the last of which was carried out by White's son. The three-gable front was present by the second expansion, while the complex layering of the rear elevation, the expansion of the kitchen wing, and the abundance of porches were developed over the course of several campaigns.

The elevations illustrate the restraint that marked the mature work of the firm. A bracketed cornice with an overscaled frieze establishes a broad, high dado that connects all thirteen gables. Other significant architectural ornaments includes fluted Doric columns, federal style entrances at front and back (with characteristically oversized dutch doors), and a Chippendale entablature above the porch. The original farmhouse and its subsequent enlargements were finished in painted clapboard until 1902, when White added the cement quoining and pebbledash.

The quoining was consistent with the Georgian derivation of the exterior trim. Pebbledash was a more unusual choice. Elaborate ornamental stucco panels and enriched mortars had appeared as decorative accents in the firm's early houses, including Tilton's and Goelet's. Naumkeag displays a related treatment in the joints of its window heads, and White specified pebbledash for the paving around Saint-Gaudens's *Standing Lincoln* in Chicago. In spite of its advantages as an architectural cladding, which included low cost, low maintenance, and long life, the firm used pebbledash to cover entire walls on only one other building, the small lodge in Hyde Park for Frederick Vanderbilt.

The original farmhouse determined the pattern of subsequent growth. Even after four major campaigns, ceiling heights were relatively low, the

front door and hallway remained in their off-center location, and the original gable had become the basic unit of expansion. With some structural help, the rest of the interior arrangement evolved independently. The large living room with its exposed steel beams was constructed with the first addition. The dining room was enlarged three times, and the stair hall was a product of the 1902 design.

The interior decor is just as eclectic as the landscape. Here the architect showed that he could achieve for himself on a budget what he would do for his clients at substantial expense. The three principal rooms—the stair hall, the living room, and the dining room—were economically but imaginatively finished and then filled with imported treasures (which he did not, or which possibly he could not, resell to his clients). The walls of the stair hall were clad in split bamboo, and the floors and staircase trimmed with

The walls and ceiling of the living room are covered by reeding, with split bamboo concealing the joints of the mats. The exposed steel was installed in the first expansion. While it was highly unusual to have such a visible means of structural support, White incorporated the beams into his decorative scheme.

celadon-glazed Guastavino tiles. Elaborately carved interior doors were recycled from a set rejected by J. P. Morgan. The rest of the effect was achieved through furniture, paintings, and fixtures. From his legendary warehouse, White supplied the limestone mantel supported by grotesque satyrs, as well as portable elements including three painted wood lions, six gilt baroque twisted columns, and a fifteenth-century French gray oak chest.

The large living room, with its walls and ceiling clad in reed matting and its wide plank wood floors, was similarly manteled and furnished. Referred to as the "Baroque Room" by the family, it is a successful venue for large and active parties, and as such expresses the program and interests of its original architect. White's son, observing that there was no place in the house where anyone would want to read a book, added the library in 1938.

The tawny old-master palette of the first two spaces is in sharp contrast

One wall of the all-white dining room consists of a monumental bay window with a continuous window seat. The child's high chair was designed by architect and family friend William Adams Delano.

to the light-filled dining room, whose entire north wall consists of a deeply undercut bay window glazed with leaded panes. The fireplace wall opposite is covered with one thousand Delft tiles arranged in a carpet-like pattern and set under a broad cornice. The remaining wall surfaces are finished with lincrusta, an imitation leather made from embossed canvas and linseed oil. Original furnishings included majolica plates, Japanese gilt lacquer temple dogs, two fifteenth-century Spanish tables, a cast-iron fireback from Versailles, and an American federal-period convex mirror. The all-white room runs counter to the prevailing taste for dark, rich tonalities. Like Rosecliff, its exact contemporary, the Box Hall dining room anticipates a shift toward a significantly lighter palette, an aesthetic that would define the work of early twentieth-century designers ranging from White's protégé Elsie de Wolfe to Charles Rennie Mackintosh.

The fireplace wall is set with a thousand Delft tiles. The dining table and chairs are late nineteenth-century reproductions of early American designs, while the range of decorative ceramics and fittings is largely European.

The "Peacock Room," tucked under the eaves on the third floor, retains its original wallpaper. The eighteenth-century Italian chairs and nineteenth-century American candle stand and gilt mirror reflect White's eclectic taste as well as his compulsion to collect beautiful objects regardless of period or style.

# James Hampden Robb House

Southampton, Long Island

1885

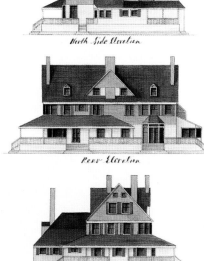

HE BIOGRAPHY of James Hampden Robb combines civic responsibility and business acumen with inherited wealth. Born in Philadelphia, he was educated in Europe, the Military School at Ossining, and Harvard. He married Cornelia Van Rensselaer Thayer of Boston in 1868 and settled in New York as a banker, cotton trader, and active participant in the local and national Democratic party. From 1882 to 1885 he was a member of the New York State Legislature where he was principally responsible for acquiring state lands to protect Niagara Falls. He helped secure the nomination of Grover Cleveland to the presidency in 1884, later rejecting Cleveland's offer of a cabinet position. In 1887 Mayor Abram S. Hewitt appointed Robb to the City Park Board, where as its president he was credited for "stubbornly opposing" the "hullabaloo and abuse" of single-minded individuals determined to encroach on green space in public parks.

Robb became thoroughly familiar with the work of McKim, Mead & White. In addition to his house in Southampton, he commissioned a city house at 22 Park Avenue in New York in 1889. As an officer of the Century Association, a private club in New York devoted to the arts, and as one of the founders of the Shinnecock Hills Golf Club, he participated in the selection of the firm to design their respective clubhouses. During the same period he must have succumbed to Stanford White's written plea for permission (and political support) to relocate the Washington Memorial Arch from Fifth Avenue into Washington Square, a controversial and highly visible encroachment on park land. As president of the Pennsylvania Society in 1907 he attempted to obtain a spot in Westminster Abbey for a memorial, designed by McKim, honoring William Penn.

Robb's Southampton house is on the western shore of Lake Agwam, simultaneously fronting on the driveway leading to First Neck Lane and on the lawn overlooking the lake, with a distant ocean view to the east. The east/west orientation of the long axis parallel to the lake eliminated the problem of a dark north lawn but did not leave much room to hide service areas.

Little was done to disguise the bulk of the large gabled box. All planes intersect at right angles, with the exception of a rounded bay at the southeast corner that contrasts with the rectangular geometry by sharply undercutting the roof above. The bay may have originally extended down to the first-floor level, repeating that contrast at the porch. The subordinate position of the service wing is reinforced by its low roof, whose broad hip recalls McKim's early interest in Bishop Berkeley's eighteenth-century Newport barn.

Rendered elevations by English cabinetmaker David Linley who has made a model of the house for the current owners.

View across Lake Agwam. The symmetrical roof massing and placement of the chimneys gives the relatively simple architecture an exceptional dignity.

On the entrance facade. the discipline of simple geometry and economical expression is softened by modest enrichments such as the bracketed cornice. The triple window on the right extends below the porch roof to illuminate the stair hall with a monumental wall of glass.

On the lake facade the integration of the chimney and the main dormer endows the massing with exceptional power and is unprecedented in the firm's work.

With its big roof, shingled upper ranges, and painted clapboard plinth, the house fits comfortably into the canon of the firm's early shingle style, but there is a greater emphasis on formal symmetry, which foreshadows the mature designs. The cross dormer establishes a dominant centerline that organizes the massing and, with its anchoring chimneys, gives the house a strong vertical lift. Continuous stringcourses connect all window heads, breaking the high walls into a disciplined composition of framed panels. The detailing is typical of the early houses, consisting of exposed ceilings at the porch, thin turned "Yankee" columns, and flat window casings.

The planning is similarly direct, reflecting the predominantly summer use of the house. Entrance is directly into the living hall, with no vestibule. The three public rooms on the ground floor—library, living room, and dining room—are connected by double pocket doors to form a continuous suite facing the lake. The first floor is surrounded by a high porch on three sides, with a separate porch at the kitchen. The upper floors fill out the footprint of the main block; most of the bedrooms face the lake.

Details are much more restrained than those of earlier designs. The entrance is a classic shingle style living hall, with a fireplace, high wall

The living room, dining room, and library all face the lake and connect en suite through wide pocket doors.

paneling, and ceiling beams framing an exposed subfloor of beaded board. The staircase animates the space. Light from the windows at the landing plays over staggered newels and tightly spaced balusters, while the orthogonal geometry of the architecture is offset by the bold graphics of the handrail.

The limited ornament and restrained details reinforce clear spatial hierarchies. The living room fireplace is decorated with a handsomely carved sunflower. The mantel in the master bedroom is integrated with a window seat overlooking the lake and the ocean, while the other bedroom fireplaces are more informal, incorporating a built-in cabinet, shelf, or mirror. Door casings at the public rooms are enhanced with entablatures; upstairs casings consist of simple reeded moldings with corner blocks. Most of the wood is now painted white, a break with the Richardsonian palette of dark, natural interiors, and possibly not original.

After Robb's death in 1911, the house was owned by his daughter and son-in-law, the architect Goodhue Livingston, and remained in the family until 1952. It was rehabilitated in 1985, during the course of which the library was reconfigured and partitions in the kitchen wing and upper floors were rearranged to add bathrooms and support spaces. Now called Dolphins, the house is privately owned.

The formal vocabulary of early shingle style living halls—stairs, beamed ceiling, fireplace—is recognizable in this subdued and dignified interior.

A curved bay and window seat in the master bedroom overlook Lake Agwam and the Atlantic beyond.

Edwin Dennison Morgan III House

# Beacon Rock

Newport, Rhode Island

1888–91

ITH ITS HULKING MASS overlooking Newport's picturesque waterfront, Beacon Rock is one of the most romantic sites on the New England coast. Well before McKim, Mead & White leveled its summit to create a plinth for the E. D. Morgan villa, the drama of the setting was recognized by the American artists who summered there in the third quarter of the nineteenth century. Landscapes such as John Kensett's 1864 *Marine Off Big Rock* celebrated the contrast of Beacon Rock's immutable granite walls with the animated play of wind, water, and light. Morgan's architects took the site as a starting point for a different dialectic, and in the process they created one of their most unusual designs.

The architect/client relationship predated the establishment of the firm. Morgan's grandfather, Edwin Dennison Morgan Sr. was the Civil War governor of New York and one of the founders of the Republican party. He may have known McKim's family through abolitionist circles and he was a close friend of White's father, Richard Grant White. In 1877 Morgan commissioned Stanford White to design a mausoleum in Hartford in col-laboration with Augustus Saint-Gaudens. The project gained a poignant immediacy in 1879 with the premature death of the governor's son, Edwin Dennison Morgan Jr. and ended tragically in 1883 with the destruction of the tomb by fire. In 1879 the twenty-three-year-old Alfred Waterman Morgan changed his name to Edwin Dennison Morgan III at the request of his grandfather, ensuring the survival of that name into the twentieth cen-tury. In 1888 and recently married, he retained McKim, Mead & White to design his Newport house on Beacon Rock.

Realized as a temple on a craggy acropolis, and accessible only by a great stone bridge, the design suggests an allegory of civilization in the wild. Classical forms rendered in smooth Callecotta marble are juxtaposed against crude masses of dark granite that were blasted from the matrix of the rock below. The art of the architecture lies in the incorporation and subsequent manipulation of the two highly dissimilar materials into the fabric of the structure itself, creating two distinct images that merge into a single house. From the sea elevations its stone walls grow straight out of the rock, while from the land approach the marble pavilions appear to sit unambiguously atop their granite base. Closer examination reveals a more intricate dia-logue, as the two materials are intertwined in a shifting figure/ground rela-tionship. At the entrance a layer of white marble columns and pediments screens a core of rough stone. On the far side of the house, the view from the highly finished interiors is framed by a semicircular apse of rough-hewn

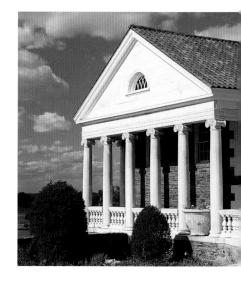

The classical pavilions that terminate the land approach to the house contrast with rough stone walls over-looking Newport Harbor.

View across the cove from Fort Adams.

Right: Ground floor plan. The broad diagonal opening to the living room has been modified in subsequent alterations, but the plan remains one of McKim, Mead & White's most original creations.

Below: The oval reception room is decorated with paintings of colonial scenes and a delicate plaster ceiling in the style of a federal period laylight.

Opposite: This view from the dining room to the living room suggests that the firm's paneled interiors were beginning to reflect academic European precedents.

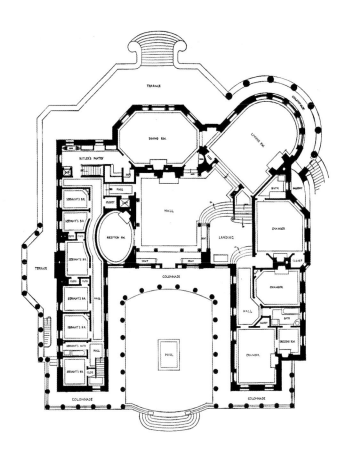

granite columns. Alternate sections of flexible clay tiles and flat roofs, in combination with heroic amounts of flashing, keep the rain off the gyrating plan below. Colonnades along both sides ease the transition from sacred temple to primitive hut.

The combination of orthogonal geometry, subtle exceptions, and violent insertions make the original plan one of the most interesting ever produced by the firm. The guest rooms and servant wings wrap symmetrically around a formal colonnade and entrance court; the slight concavity over the front door foreshadows the pyrotechnics that lie beyond. Columns lining the front hall repeat the layering of the exterior and reinforce, if only for a moment, the genteel regularity of the plan up to that point. A metaphoric explosion in the corner blasts an opening between the hall and the living room, nearly amputating that space from the underlying geometry to create a major diagonal axis towards the view of Newport harbor. The scale of that single gesture overwhelms the house and is virtually unprecedented in American architecture. Other plan devices, such as the bending of the broad stair treads, the superimposition of the oval reception room on the servants' corridor, and the slight axial shift of the octagonal dining room, reflect the secondary consequences of the principal gesture and create a plan that delights at every level of detail. The firm would never again embrace such a dramatic manipulation of exterior form and interior space.

While the great freedom of the plan connects Beacon Rock to earlier shingle style designs by the firm and their contemporaries, the interiors reveal the growing preference by 1890 for the architectural decoration of Georgian England. White's proto art nouveau extravagances, and even McKim's modest colonial details, are banished in favor of raised walnut paneling, fluted pilasters, and dentilled cornices. The historic scenes on the walls of the reception room acknowledge Morgan's American heritage, while the elaborate Adamesque ceilings on the second floor imply an equal measure of English noble bearings.

Morgan was a satisfied client. While Beacon Rock was still under construction, he retained McKim, Mead & White to design a manor house in Wheatley Hills, Long Island. Between 1890 and 1900 the firm expanded the Long Island house with an assortment of shingled, colonial revival farm buildings and residential structures to create a fully integrated country estate of remarkable dimensions. Morgan's family occupied Beacon Rock until about 1925. For many years it was the home and studio of Felix de Welden, sculptor of the Iwo Jima monument in Washington, D.C. The house remains privately owned.

Stair hall. Guest rooms were located off the landing, with family bedrooms upstairs. The current entry to the living room is visible under the stairs.

# Samuel Longstreth Parrish House

Southampton, Long Island

1889

AMUEL LONGSTRETH PARRISH was the client for this attractive essay in summer architecture. He must have been a remarkable individual, possessing athletic, artistic, and commercial interests to a degree rarely combined in a single person. He was considered Southampton's "first citizen" for the number of civic projects he initiated or sustained. In 1891 he and five other friends, including McKim, Mead & White clients Charles Atterbury, Edward S. Mead, and J. Hampden Robb, created America's first organized golf club in the Shinnecock Hills, retaining the firm to design the clubhouse. Parrish was a collector of paintings, and in 1897 he conceived of a public art museum for the emerging resort. He hired architect Grosvenor Atterbury (who was Charles's son as well as a former McKim, Mead & White apprentice) to design a gallery in the center of Southampton, and Olmsted to create the arboretum and sculpture garden on the adjoining land. Parrish later hired Atterbury to design a commercial block opposite the Parrish Art Museum, creating the picturesque buildings that anchor Southampton's retail center today.

Pencil marks on this photograph from the McKim, Mead & White office archives show that the architects were reconsidering the design of the smaller flanking dormers even after construction was completed. (Collection of The New-York Historical Society)

Parrish was born in Philadelphia and attended Exeter and Harvard, graduating in 1870. He studied law and practiced in Philadelphia before moving to New York in 1877. Parrish remained a bachelor until he was seventy-nine, and for the last thirty years of his life he lived in the Captain Rogers house, an eighteenth-century clapboard residence and one-time boarding house in which McKim had spent the summer of 1887 as a paying guest. Parrish's keen interest in Southampton was limited to weekends and summers. He maintained an office at 25 Broad Street in New York well after his retirement in 1897 and a house at 825 Fifth Avenue until his death in 1932 from injuries sustained in an automobile accident.

In 1889 he commissioned McKim, Mead & White to design a new house on Southampton's First Neck Lane, a block away from his brother James C. Parrish, who shared his civic zeal and organizational abilities. Samuel Parrish may not have spent much time in this house. His mother lived there until her death in 1895, after which he sold it to his sister.

The Parrish house sits on one of the most attractive country roads on Long Island. Parallel to the street, the building and its long front porch

The slight projection of the second-story window bays at each corner is an extremely subtle visual device for strengthening the corner.

The form and detailing of the stair bring a high level of style to a simple design.

The emerging vocabulary of the colonial revival style— symmetry, balance of wall and roof, and touches of rich classical ornament—is evident in this view across the front porch.

overlook a well-defined rectangular front yard, similar in proportion to the main elevation and roughly four times its size. The original site plan featured a sweeping driveway centered on the entrance gable. With this device, all of the principal decorative features of the house are combined to enhance the choreography of arrival, forming a continuous and delightful sequence: the smooth green front lawn; the exuberant finialed dormer in the center of the roof; the generously (but not overly) scaled cornices, moldings, and columns; the combination of straight, round, and gabled porches; and the entrance itself with its extra-wide door and delicate elliptical window. The composition establishes a dialogue between house, open space, and street that is a paradigm of the simultaneously public and private nature of the best suburban domestic architecture. McKim, Mead & White never abandoned its keen sense of urbanism, even outside the city. The original white

Dining room. The open planning typical of the earlier houses is replaced by an arrangement of separate rooms connected by small doorways.

fence, now gone, must have had gates at either end.

The ground floor is arranged as separate rooms with very little formal circulation. The compact front hall opens onto the living and dining rooms through wide openings, allowing easy communication between public rooms, while the kitchen and a billiard room are concealed behind offsets for greater privacy. The lively, ornamental staircase extends the flow of space to the bedrooms on the second floor.

The Parrish house illustrates the synthesis of American federalist, Long Island vernacular, high Victorian, and Greek revival elements typical of the later wood houses of McKim, Mead & White, as well as the emerging classicism that characterized all of the firm's work after 1887. The broad roofs and sawtooth gables of the earlier designs are here replaced by a shallow hip roof

and an unbroken cornice, redirecting the emphasis from the protective shelter of the canopy toward the dignified composition of the walls. That change in architectural expression, which first appears in the 1885 H. A. C. Taylor house in Newport, signaled the firm's move toward Georgian and classical prototypes and away from the spirited combination of Yankee vernacular and aesthetic exoticism of the early designs. Yet the Parrish house is anything but academic in its execution. The front door is not centered on the entrance gable, the staircase cuts the elliptical window in half, and the roof at the north corner overhangs the wall below by four feet. The trim vision of compactness, symmetry, and public visibility presented at the main facade is contradicted at the back by an enormous and rambling extension, which doubles the size of the house as it encloses a truly private rear yard.

Living room (left)
and pantry.

# King Model Houses

New York

1891–92

THE THIRTY-TWO ROWHOUSES and one apartment building designed in 1891 for David H. King Jr. illustrate McKim, Mead & White's skill at integrating multiple structures into coherent designs at an urban scale. Like the Villard Houses begun nine years earlier, the expression of individual units is subordinated to a unified facade. Here the unfolded street elevation is almost one thousand feet in length and realized as an urban palace in the firm's characteristic style of the 1890s. The block could have been one of the sights that led Le Corbusier to declare that only after seeing the work of McKim, Mead & White in New York did he fully appreciate the architecture of the Italian Renaissance. In the case of the King Model Houses, the intended occupants were neither Florentine princes nor wealthy American gentry but middle-class families who could afford to pay eighty to one hundred sixty dollars per month for a six-bedroom house.

The developer, David H. King Jr., was a civic-minded contractor whose portfolio included some of the period's most significant monuments and whose career was closely and even personally connected to Stanford White's. He retained the firm for six separate commissions, ranging from an unbuilt project in Washington, D.C., to Premium Point, his country house in New Rochelle. Along the way he constructed White's Washington Memorial Arch at the base of Fifth Avenue as well as the critically successful but financially troubled Madison Square Garden, in which he was a major investor and active partner. He was also the contractor for Richard Morris Hunt's pedestal for the Statue of Liberty. King's collaborations with the best architects of the period must have come from an innate degree of taste that is not normally associated with real estate investments; in 1891 he commissioned three excellent firms to contribute to his most ambitious project, the King Model Houses in Harlem.

Harlem had become the focus of feverish speculative development after the 1884 extension of the Eighth Avenue elevated rapid transit to

Opposite: The block-long facade sits on a continuously rusticated base and is punctuated by the regular rhythm of balconies, canopies, and front doors. Window surrounds of molded ironspot brick and medallions in matching terra-cotta (above) mark the drawing room of each unit.

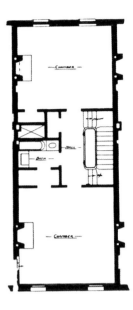

145th Street. Operating on a scale larger than most of his rivals, King purchased nine acres of land with four full block frontages on 138th and 139th Streets. He built almost two hundred dwellings on this site, retaining McKim, Mead & White for the design of the northernmost frontage. Other blocks were assigned to the partnership of Bruce Price and Clarence S. Luce, who designed the two back-to-back rows to the south, while James Brown Lord completed the southernmost block along 138th Street. The results of the collaboration are as notable for the overall harmony of the ensemble as for the distinction of each firm's contribution.

The typical structure was a single-family dwelling, generally four stories in height, ranging from seventeen to twenty-two feet wide. In most designs the small apartment buildings were along the avenues; no structure was allowed to break the uniform cornice line. Rear yards were developed as service areas facing alleys, along the model of Philadelphia or Boston— a planning device intended to keep "the business part of housekeeping" out of sight. Contemporary marketing materials emphasized the value as well as the details of home ownership, including "sanitary perfection," substantial construction ("nothing flimsy or gingerbread"), abundance of sunlight, and various amenities, including an unusually high number of closets. Most important, there was an implied guarantee of a foolproof investment. King even offered mortgage life insurance to reassure the cautious and placed restrictions on each title to protect all homeowners from "adjoining nuisances."

White was the partner in charge of most of the firm's commercial and residential work. The King Model Houses, which are a bit of both, are generally credited to him. His design combines overall restraint with controlled bursts of architectural ornament. The rusticated brownstone base stretches from avenue to avenue, surmounted by three-story walls clad in iron-spot brick. The scale of the block is broken up by setbacks, mid-block arcades, quoining, and hyphens connecting major parts. Divisions between units are expressed in the regular rhythm of balconies and canopies, while the facades of individual houses are animated by asymmetrical doorways, juxtapositions of large and small openings, and multiple designs for window surrounds. The large centering medallions are particularly fine examples of architectural terra-cotta and represent one of the firm's many successful collaborations with the Perth Amboy Terra Cotta Company.

The interiors show the designer's sure touch, although the scale is diminutive compared to the firm's houses for the wealthy. In keeping with the commercial nature of the enterprise, the details are more a tribute to

The columns, built-in seats, and spatial layering that were a part of the firm's standard vocabulary for larger houses give the entrance hall equal measures of intimacy, grandeur, and complexity. All of the interiors illustrated are from the residence of Mr. and Mrs. E. Randy Dupree.

manufacturing than to hand work. Walls are covered with lincrusta, decorated with molded plaster cornices, and hung with mirrors in elaborately machined frames. The effect is extremely charming. The benches, alcove, and fireplace of the reception room recall the firm's shingle style living halls of a decade earlier. Twin Corinthian columns and twisted balusters, which bracket a built-in seat connecting the dining room to the parlor on the second floor, create a tableau that for an instant combines the grandeur of McKim, Mead & White's palaces of the 1890s with the intimacy of their earliest cottages. The heralded "sanitary perfection" consisted of one full bath to be shared by all six bedrooms and one additional water closet, the latter accessible only from the rear yard and probably intended for the servants.

The hall
on the second floor
features a second pair of
composite columns
framing a built-in seat.
The stair rail is supported
by alternating patterns of
twisted balusters.

The King Model Houses proved a poor investment for the developer and the buyers, as the Panic of 1904 caused the real estate market to collapse and delivered a blow to Harlem from which it has yet to recover. In the ensuing decline most of the original residents sold their homes, frequently at heavy losses, and families of recent immigrants moved into the area. Amid a general retreat of property values, the King Model Houses developed a certain cachet, particularly along the McKim, Mead & White block, which attracted a population of prominent black professionals. Those upwardly mobile residents became identified with their tenacious pursuit of the social order that inspired the original development, giving rise to the name Striver's Row by which the block is known today.

The elaborate moldings that decorate the walls and ceilings of the drawing room may have been selected by an enthusiastic plasterer. The cornice and fireplace reveal McKim, Mead & White's sure hand with architectural decoration.

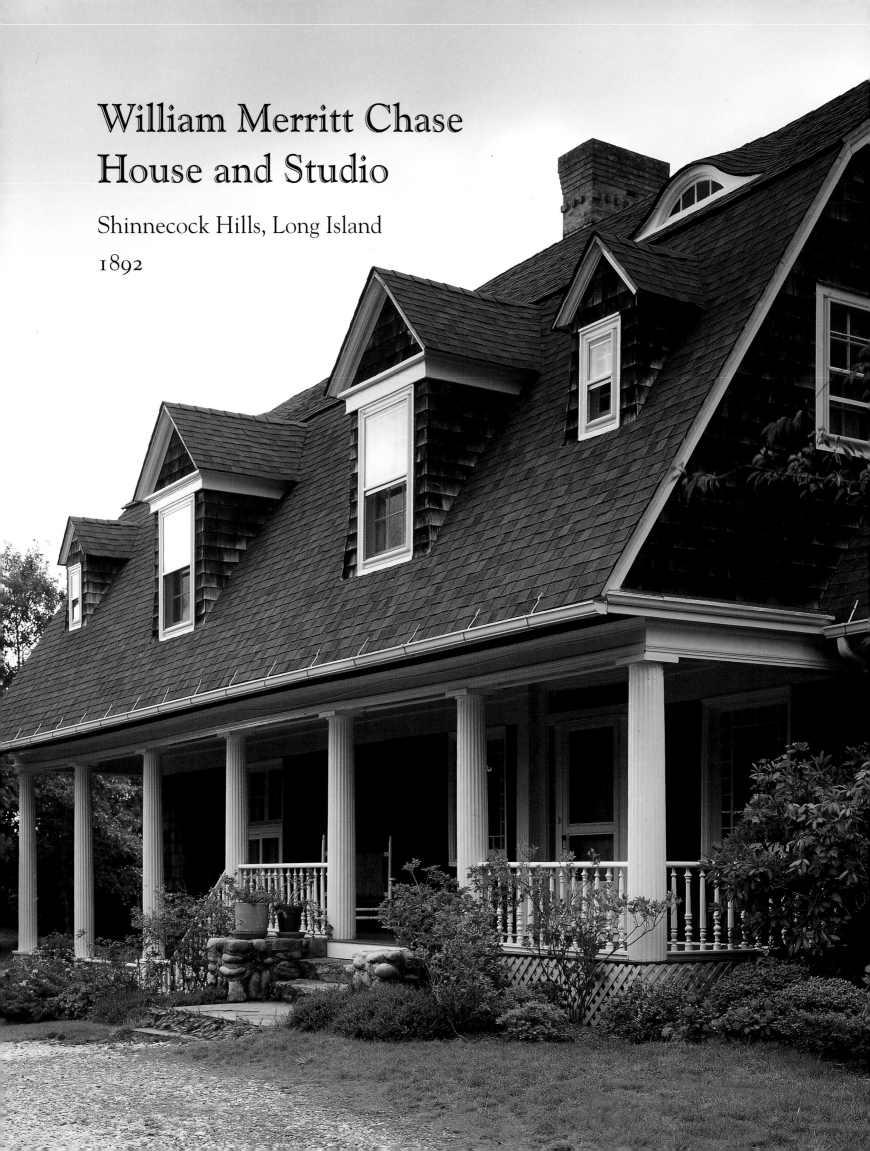

# William Merritt Chase
# House and Studio

Shinnecock Hills, Long Island

1892

N 1891, WILLIAM MERRITT CHASE was persuaded to leave New York during the summer to offer painting classes on Long Island's East End. His benefactors, Mrs. William S. Hoyt and Mrs. Henry Porter, enlisted Samuel L. Parrish and Charles L. Atterbury to put up the land for the school, while the two women recruited the students, established the schedule, and, as a further incentive, obtained a separate site for a house in Shinnecock Hills, three miles east of Southampton. By 1892 Chase was living in a modest cottage with an attached studio, illustrated in a rendering produced by the office of McKim, Mead & White but for which no record of any commission from Chase himself exists. There is a suggestion that this house was originally designed for Atterbury and later modified for the artist. In either case, the appearance of the finished house and the relationship of Chase to the architects support the traditional attribution as an "off-the-books" design of McKim, Mead & White.

The office discouraged "off-the-books" work. Because McKim was aware of the need to maintain tight financial controls, the firm's original partnership agreement of June 21, 1880, stipulated "All receipts to be banked." White was perpetually designing monuments, picture frames, lamps, and magazine covers that were not always recorded in the office records, but he billed clients directly and deposited their payments in the firm's account. The three partners cannot have avoided "pro-bono" architecture on a formal or an informal basis, producing the occasional drawing for a church, a charity, or a friend. White drew beautifully and rapidly and was as likely to answer a request with a plan and an elevation as with a business letter. Some of those favors turned into buildings. A similar chain of events may have occurred here.

Chase and White were friends and contemporaries. Both were members of the Century Association, which was open to "amateurs of the arts," as well as the more exclusive Tile Club, whose membership was limited to sympathetic artists of the American Renaissance including Sargent, Dewing,

The gambrel roof, which the firm had used in some of their earliest houses, was commodious, informal, and a natural addition to the Shinnecock landscape.

Although convention holds that facades should never have an odd number of columns, this unusual elevation allows the family quarters and the studio beyond to have equally important entrances.

Renderings such as this were a standard part of the firm's design process in the 1890s. (Avery Architectural and Fine Arts Library, Columbia University)

and La Farge. White's biographer Charles Baldwin quotes an 1888 letter in which a year-old loan from White is repaid by the grateful painter. In a 1906 interview with the Paris *Herald,* Chase praised the recently deceased architect as "a man thoroughly alive, an artist to his fingertips." Baldwin also says that White "suggested" the design for the house. The firm must have assigned a draftsman to prepare the rendering and to work out the details, because the design of any house is too complex and the design of this one is too good to have been completed over dinner.

At the time the house was built, Shinnecock was open farmland. The site at the top of a gentle hill afforded unobstructed views of the bays and ocean beyond. In this summery context the house appears frequently in Chase's paintings, most memorably in *The Bayberry Bush* of about 1895. It may have been the ultimate family house. The Chases' albums are filled with pictures of their eight children posing in costume, picnicking on the lawn, and playing on the porch. Chase had a special banner he would hoist to announce the birth of each child; at some point the attic was rebuilt to create more bedrooms. The house was sold after Chase's death in 1916 (one subsequent owner was the niece of Samuel Parrish). It is still a private dwelling and is virtually unchanged, although the open fields have filled in with trees. The studio fireplace and the kitchen extension are additions, and other spaces have been the subject of very minor modifications; the original plan site included a stable.

The two-story living hall was the heart of the house. When Chase lived there its beaded board walls were covered with paintings and other treasures from his collection of studio props.

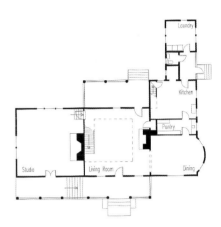

Ground floor plan.
The fireplace in the studio
was a later addition.
(Courtesy Buttrick White &
Burtis Architects)

It is not hard to see why White and his partners were willing to design this project for free, as the combination of a house and a studio is in itself an interesting architectural problem. It allows the expression of two different scales and the accommodation of two different activities—living and working—in a single building, requiring the designer to resolve the program's inherent tension within a single harmonious composition. In the Chase house the functional separation is accomplished by an inconspicuous door off the living hall and a change of level. Each division is distinguished by different sizes and types of windows. The resolution of the whole was achieved by aligning the studio with the rest of the plan, by cladding all surfaces in unpainted shingles, and by subordinating all exceptions, including the swelling dining room bay and the recessed second-floor balcony, to the embrace of the roof. The change of scale of the front porch as it steps down to follow the hill foreshadows a similar change of scale within, but ironically the living hall, not the studio, is the major interior space.

The image of the house is dominated by its large gambrel roof. That form appears on McKim, Mead & White buildings from the early 1880s in connection with their Newport work, where it was a standard feature of the town's disappearing stock of eighteenth-century buildings. On a bare hilltop in Long Island farm country it was a particularly felicitous choice, and the firm used the same roof for the Shinnecock Hills Golf Club. Gambrels have a practical basis as they maximize the habitable area on the upper floor while allowing the building to sit lower to the ground. They are certainly picturesque and, as we have seen, they can accommodate extra bedrooms. Chase's house has a tightly staggered and interlocking triple roof that organizes the minor irregularities of the plan below.

In keeping with their client's limited means, the extent and design of the exterior ornament is restrained. Most of the decorative activity derives

The great rubble stone fireplace dominates the living hall, which was the most important family room. The dining room (above) was the only other public space.

from massing, painted trim, and a variety of window shapes and glass divisions, including leaded glass sidelights at the front door. Enriched detail was limited to fluted columns with rope-like capitals, and highly figurative porch railings, which were always painted white.

The interior reveals an intense singularity of space and material. The plan on both levels is wrapped around an enormous two-story living hall, while every wall and ceiling of every room is covered with beaded board. Architectural richness is introduced through the massive stone fireplace in the living hall, the handsomely carved and polished staircase, and the medallions on the beaded board ceiling. In Chase's day the walls of the studio were hung with fabric, and the living room was filled with paintings. The newel post served as a base for a small cast of *Winged Mercury*, and a giant Chinese parasol stood by the front door. Chase's collection followed the architecture of his house, mixing the delicate with the rough, the monumental with the humanly scaled, and the everyday with the exotic, all combinations that suggest the active participation of Stanford White.

Master bedroom and dressing room (above) and a dormer in a child's bedroom. The walls and ceilings of all upstairs rooms are finished in beaded board.

## Mrs. Joseph Bloomfield Wetherill House

# Head of the Harbor

St. James, Long Island

1894–95

HE OCTAGONAL MASS of Head of the Harbor is among the most memorable images in the canon of McKim, Mead & White's country houses. Built in 1895, its classically inspired elevations are a paradigm of the colonial revival vocabulary that had emerged from the firm's shingle style architecture of the previous decade.

Stanford White worked on houses for three of his wife's sisters, including Katherine Smith Wetherill, for whom he designed this unusual villa at the summit of a steep hill overlooking St. James Harbor. Her husband, Reverend Joseph Bloomfield Wetherill, had died in 1886, leaving Kate with two children. With the death of their mother in 1890, Kate Wetherill and her sisters came into a significant inheritance from their great-aunt Cornelia Clinch Stewart, widow of the department store magnate A. T. Stewart, Kate had the excuse as well as the means to reorganize her household at the same time Stanford and Bessie White were enlarging Box Hill. Her brother-in-law agreed to provide the design of the house at cost. The completed estate, including its stone viaduct and entrance gates, shingled outbuildings, and boat dock, comprised eighty acres.

The octagonal main block dominates views of the house from all directions. Its distinctive form also establishes the theme of the interior, which is characterized by alternating efforts to resist the underlying geometry and to celebrate it. At the ground floor the principal walls are aligned into a cruciform plan, with porches encircling the house and filling the negative spaces left by the overlap of the two geometries. The upper walls, each surmounted by a peaked roof, fill out the octagon and create a pinwheel of gables. Before the original roof of the service wing was changed from a gambrel and raised one and a half stories, the effect of the saw-toothed profile must have been even more striking.

As with any Long Island estate near the Sound, the approach is from the south and the view is to the north. Here the strong figure of a house-(almost)-in-the-round, combined with the steep hill falling away on all

The colonial revival style achieves grammatical and geometric perfection at Head of the Harbor.

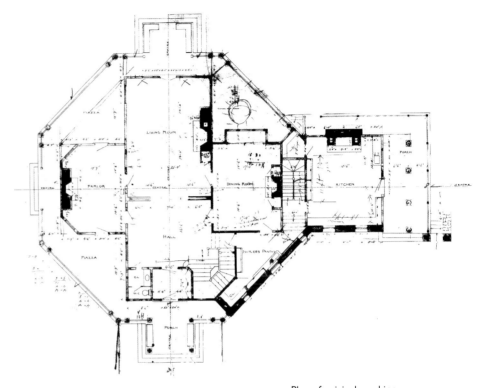

Plan of original working drawing. Pencil marks, possibly in White's hand, show that he was not fully satisfied with the arrangement of the dining room.

Opposite: The house is perched on the top of a hill, with a steep descent to St. James Harbor.

The major axis through the center of the house connects the entry court to the living room via a series of carefully detailed openings.

sides, eliminates the usual problem of a dark north lawn. In fact, there is no space alongside the house for a conventionally planned landscape, so the flower garden had to be incorporated into the entrance court and the croquet lawn located at the bottom of the hill, connected to the house by an outdoor stair of more than one hundred steps.

While the octagon was the perfect device for such a uniformly precipitous site, its geometry was an unusual choice for any serious designer of the period. The three partners may have come across a regional tradition of octagonal houses on their New England journeys. At the same time they could not have ignored its arch reference to the 1854 Yankee self-help book by Orson Squire Fowler called *An Octagon House: A Home For All*, which touted the "practical" advantages of octagonal houses ("contains one fifth more floor area for its wall"), as well as their capacity for moral and physical refreshment.

Aside from its unusual massing, the exterior of the house is representative of wood-framed dwellings of the mature style of the firm after 1890.

The twisted newel and balusters recall the pulpit in the Sabbatarian Meeting House in Newport.

Decorative elements in the living room include Dutch tile, classical moldings, embroidered fringe, and tapestries of arcadian landscapes.

Only the third floor fully acknowledges the octagonal form of the house. The balcony opens to the second floor hall; the stair ascends to the widow's walk on the roof.

Shingled walls and simple roof lines are decorated with high-style classical details picked out in white paint: enriched cornices, delicately mullioned windows, an urn-topped widow's walk, and fluted Ionic columns supporting the wrap-around porch. Doric capitals outside the kitchen door confirmed the subordinate status of the service wing, a subtlety that may not have been universally appreciated. The academic vocabulary of the elevations is animated by the use of natural materials and the juxtapositions of opposites: thick and thin, rough and smooth, delicate and massive. The oversized dutch door is framed by elegant leaded glass sidelights and federal style tracery in the oval wooden sash. Palladian windows with elaborate frames sparkle against broad planes of shingles. Foundations and chimneys are laid up with granite boulders left by the glacier that originally formed Long Island. Their visual weight as well as their indigenous color and texture anchor the house to its site and endow its architecture with a distinctively regional flavor.

The interior planning reflects the compact program of a summer house as well as the modest needs of a minister's widow, albeit a fairly well-to-do one. The cruciform ground floor is organized around major and minor cross axes, with a constant emphasis on the controlled flow of space. The path from the front door leads in a continuous straight line through overscaled openings to the hall, the living room, and ultimately to the porch overlooking the harbor. The dining room and parlor are set off to the side, their relative privacy protected by more normally scaled doorways placed off axis. Like the elevations, the interior decorative scheme is a mixture of plain and fancy. Most rooms are finished in smooth plaster and decorated with traditional mantels, baseboards, and cornices. In the living room, fluted pilasters with egg-and-dart capitals support a beamed ceiling and frame panels of tapestries and an elaborately tiled fireplace. A replica of the exuberant twisted newel post that McKim photographed in Newport's Sabbatarian Meeting House marks the ascent of the main stair to the upper floors.

The planning of the second floor continues to flirt with the dominant shape of the house, but the final layout is decidedly orthogonal. Halls and bedrooms are realized as near-rectangles with the help of half bays and lots of triangular closets. Only the third floor fully acknowledges the geometry of the exterior as guest rooms open onto an octagonal hall whose octagonal balcony is centered under an eight-faceted dome and matching skylight. A vertiginous stair ascends from the third floor to the widow's walk at the intersection of the eight gables, forty feet above the driveway and two hundred feet above the harbor, where Dr. Wetherill's widow could appreciate the panoramic view of Long Island's North Shore and Connecticut in the distance.

A rustic teahouse at the foot of the hill linked the dock beyond to the main house above. The use of thatch for the roof was as effective as it was unusual. (Collection of The New-York Historical Society)

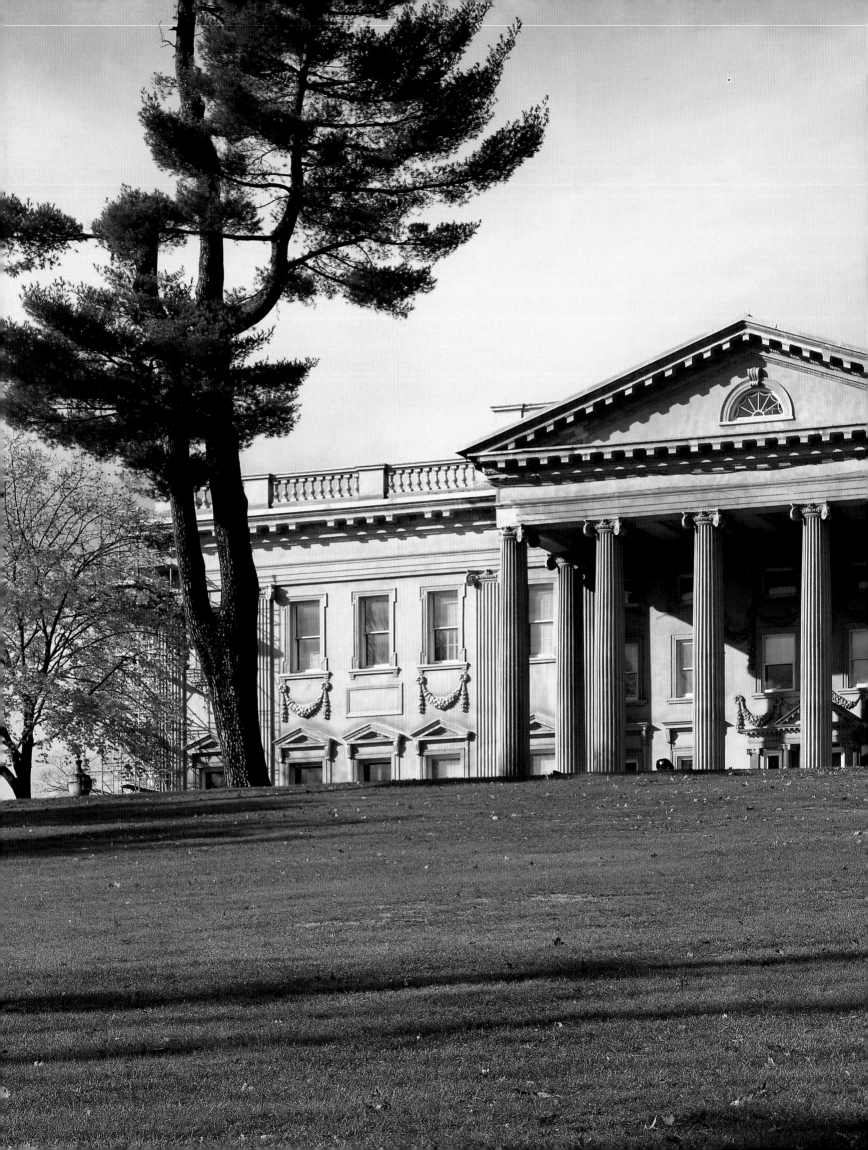

Ogden Mills House

# Staatsburgh

Staatsburg, New York

1895–97

 REMARKABLE NUMBER of McKim, Mead & White's residential commissions were for alterations to existing houses, suggesting that they worked for old money as well as new. One of these commissions was for Ogden Mills. Although his money was not by any means ancient (his father, Darius Ogden Mills, had made an enormous fortune from the 1849 California gold rush), Mills was married to Ruth Livingston, whose family had been prominent in the Hudson Valley since the seventeenth century. As a couple they combined unimpeachable Knickerbocker lineage with bottomless resources and a willingness to spend them, a profile that would eventually make Ruth Livingston Mills a leading (though ultimately unsuccessful) candidate to succeed Caroline Schermerhorn Astor as the doyenne of New York society.

The Millses had already built a town house at 2 East Sixty-Ninth Street, designed by Richard Morris Hunt (the reigning architect to the very rich), when in 1890 Mrs. Mills inherited a twenty-five-room Greek revival house in the Hudson Valley, built in 1832 by her great-grandfather, Morgan Lewis. In 1895, when the Millses decided to modify their country house for entertaining during the fall season, Hunt was in failing health. Possibly at the suggestion of his brother-in-law Whitelaw Reid, for whom McKim, Mead & White had recently completed two celebrated houses, Mills retained the younger firm to enlarge Staatsburgh, with White as the partner in charge.

The Millses wanted to impress at every level, from the winding driveway, which provides tantalizing and well-framed views of the monumental

Two rooms in the old house were sacrificed to create this imperial staircase. The ceiling above the tapestry contains an allegorical painting of equal magnificence.

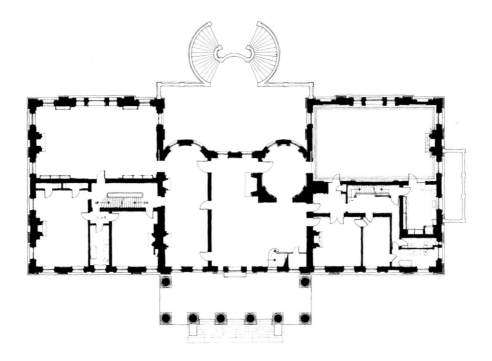

Ground floor plan. Morgan Lewis's grand chambers became anterooms to the new library, terrace, and dining room, which are aligned on the river side of the house. (Courtesy Jan Hird Pokorny Architects).

entrance, to the elevated terrace overlooking the Hudson, and all spaces in between. The architects added the new front porch, replaced older parts of the building with new two-story wings to the north and south, and painted the stucco structure in the manner of Nash's Regents Park terraces. Consciously or not, the composition of the entrance facade is strongly reminiscent of the White House, which the firm was to rebuild seven years later.

In order to accommodate new public rooms of appropriate dimension, the wings were constructed with considerably higher ceilings than the twelve feet that had been sufficient for Morgan Lewis. The juxtaposition of room sizes establishes a dialogue between the older and newer parts of the house in plan, section, and elevation, and the marriage of the two scales reveals the architects' masterful command of space making, classical design, and residential planning. The smaller openings of the 1832 structure play off against the monumental order of the new porch; the half levels required to join the structure at the upper floors allow for subtle distinctions among interior zones; and the ceiling height in the older spaces simply enhances the impact of the new dining room and its twin, the new library.

The house is the perfect architectural expression of the taste of wealthy, cultivated, and powerful American families in the late nineteenth century. The decorative scheme of the new rooms celebrates the abundance and beauty of the North American continent and, thanks to portraits of dozens of Mrs. Mills's colonial ancestors, the prominent role the Livingstons played in its evolution. White brought in Allard & Fils from Paris for the execution of the new rooms. While it is not clear how much of the interiors was designed by the architects, their complex allegories and tailored iconography could only have been dreamed up by someone who was intimately familiar with the Millses' background, ambition, and self-esteem.

At the same time Staatsburgh (as the house was known in the Mills era) is an important document in the social history of its period. More than any other house by McKim, Mead & White, the Mills mansion illustrates the complex equation of circulation and adjacencies that made up the program of the country house in the Victorian era, particularly as applied to the choreography of entertainment, the segregation of sleeping quarters, and the role of the senior administrator in the management of the household.

A sconce and mirrored door in the dining room.

The ground floor was designed for dinner parties. With the principal rooms arranged enfilade, guests processed from the hall north along the main axis, passing through a small assembly room before entering the new dining room with its marble walls, gilded fittings, trompe l'oeil ceilings, and tapestries of nature in bloom. After dinner they reversed their path through the hall to a drawing room that had been created out of two parlors in the 1832 block. The ladies were left for a short period while the gentlemen descended to the billiard room for manly refreshment. Later the guests would reunite for coffee, which required following the axis to its southern terminus in the new library, whose decoration included images of Native Americans swathed in pearls.

The windows of the original house were transformed into doors to the new wings This opening connects an 1832 reception room to the new dining room.

The requirements for sleeping quarters were no less rigorous. Unmarried female guests slept in the old part of the house in the middle of the second floor, just off the main stairs. Married couples slept in the north wing, protecting and yet separated from the maidens by the half flight of stairs required by the higher ceiling in the dining room below. The Millses' two daughters occupied the matching suite over the library, with the same half level of separation and the same guardian role. Bachelors were quartered a full two flights below, next to the billiard and gun rooms. The back stairs that connected the bachelors' quarters to the rooms above also ran past the first-floor bedroom of Ruth Livingston Mills, who undoubtedly reminded all guests of her reputation as a light sleeper.

Ruth Livingston Mills's bedroom in the southeast corner of the ground floor.

It took at least one additional character to guarantee order. Mr. Hoyt, who served as Mr. Mills's personal secretary, occupied the ground-floor bedroom next to the service stair at the other end of the house. By day he could command the kitchen and its silver safe (to which only he and Mr. Mills knew the combination) as well as consult with Mrs. Mills in the adjacent room she used as her office. In the evenings he mingled with the guests, but by night he was able to monitor traffic on the back staircase leading to the maids' bedrooms on the third floor. At the same time he guarded a second and even more enormous safe into which arriving guests were required to deposit their jewelry, and from which they could retrieve it only for dinner and at departure.

In 1938 Gladys Mills Phipps gave the house and furnishings to the State of New York as a memorial to her parents. The exterior is currently undergoing a long period of restoration, sponsored by the New York State Department of Parks, Recreation, and Historic Preservation. The house is open to the public.

Upstairs guest bathroom. The architectural language of modern bathrooms was in its infancy in 1895.

The pantry with the silver safe flanked by the dumbwaiter. A printed notice on the opposite wall spelled out a dress code for the servants.

# Charles Williams and George Williams Houses

Buffalo, New York
1895–96 and 1895–99

ITHIN A SPAN OF FOUR MONTHS, Charles and George Williams commissioned separate houses on adjoining lots on Delaware Avenue, the best address in Buffalo. Charles, a banker, contacted McKim, Mead & White in February 1895 and was in residence the following year. George, whose fortune came from tanneries, initiated his house on the more prominent corner site in the following June. He would end up spending twice as much as his older brother and taking twice as long to complete his own project. In spite of a significant difference in cost, the two houses are remarkably similar in the details of their execution, and together they illustrate McKim, Mead & White's stylish response to the design of a villa in a mid-urban, garden setting.

By the turn of the century, Buffalo was the seventh largest city in the United States and a major industrial and agricultural center supported by the influx of thousands of European immigrants. Its business leaders possessed a high level of civic pride, expressed in a series of ambitious urban improvements, beginning with Olmsted's 1868 vision for an extensive network of parks and parkways and culminating in the Pan American Exposition of 1901. They also took advantage of the city's wealth of material resources and skilled labor to create civic and personal architectural statements of unusually high quality.

Buffalo's Gold Coast lay along the hill to the north of the city, with Delaware Avenue as its main thoroughfare. In 1868 Richardson designed a Second Empire house for William Dorsheimer at number 438, near the base of the hill. North Street, which crossed Delaware Avenue at the top of the hill, was the other desirable address. McKim, Mead & White had built a steeply gabled shingle style villa there in 1882 for Edwin Metcalf. After the transformation of Delaware Avenue into Buffalo's great boulevard, the tide flowed uphill past North Street, filling progressively bigger lots than Dorsheimer's and Metcalf's with mansions that were considerably more ambitious than Richardson's or his former protégés' efforts of the previ-

The marble threshold at the front door of Charles Williams's house is carved with the name of his architects.

The two-story porch at the front door of the Charles Williams house addresses Delaware Avenue with a directness that is simultaneously welcoming and intimidating.

ous decades. The standard program for these new villas-on-the-outskirts included an imposing house, a formal driveway, and a carriage house, plus lawns and gardens.

In 1894 Robert Root retained McKim, Mead & White to design a gambrel-roofed, red brick Georgian mansion on the southwest corner of Delaware Avenue and North Street, gateway to the new boulevard district. The Williams brothers, who were connected to Root by marriage, transformed Buffalo's most fashionable corner into a family compound by building across the street. The presence of four houses around such a visible location gave rise to a local perception that McKim, Mead & White were Buffalo architects.

The Williams houses are loosely based on English and Italian neoclassical prototypes, with high brick walls enhanced by broad cornices, regularly spaced windows, and stone trim. Their roofs, the defining characteristic of earlier McKim, Mead & White houses, are suppressed and formal emphasis is placed on two-story porches of truly imperial splendor. This element appears frequently in the firm's work after the World's Columbian Exposition of 1893, and the mid-nineties can be seen as the firm's giant column phase. White even drew up a scheme for transforming the gabled front of his own house, Box Hill, into a monumental porch supported on twenty-foot fluted Corinthian columns.

The planning and design of the Buffalo houses explores the issues posed by their setting in that city's garden district. The intermediate density found outside the city center encouraged development of a freestanding villa in a miniature park, but the district's proximity to and affiliation with the center of town created a strong urban context. Here the problem is largely resolved with landscape elements. Massive iron fences on stone bases hold the line of the street and delineate the limits of each private park, while elaborate brick piers mark significant entrances to the grounds.

The scallop shell motif reappears above the front door.

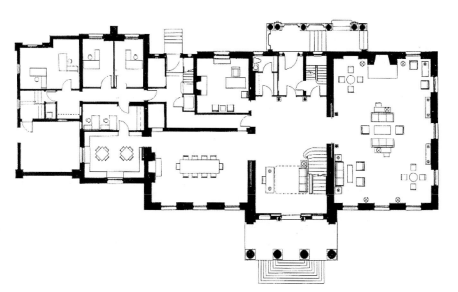

Ground floor plan of the George Williams house. (Courtesy Hamilton, Houston, Lownie, Architects)

The porches that dominate the elevations connect each house to the life of the street, but do not always indicate the location of the front door. The problem is specific to the building type and to this day has never been fully solved. Town and country houses are designed with one main entrance, but the mid-urban villa often needs two. With the city so close and the rituals of hospitality so much a part of organized social life, provision had to be made for the visitor who appeared on foot, even if the owner and most guests arrived by carriage. The side door with its high stoop had become the principal point of entry, protected from the weather with a suitably cere-monial enclosure. In Charles Williams's house the carriage entrance on the north side duplicates the front door on the east side facing the street; both are covered by grand porches, and the architects had to struggle inside the house to connect the side door to the front hall. In George's house the side door and the front door are one and the same, and the commanding porch that overlooks the city on the south facade is purely rhetorical.

To create an interior scale that fulfilled the expectations generated by the elevations, both houses are organized around enormous living halls, with massive, rectangular staircases leading to the bedroom floors. The balance of the interiors are tightly planned, with space on the first floor at a premium. One house has a small second-floor library at the head of the stairs; the other includes a rather unconvincing ballroom in the basement. But typically the ground floor had to accommodate all public rooms plus essential support spaces. Town houses permitted public rooms to be spread over multiple floors, while country houses provided unlimited space at the ground level. In their compact arrangement each of the Williams's houses, though vast by con-temporary standards, illustrates the planning limitations of the garden villa.

The level of finishes is exceptionally high. Mosaic paving, marble pilasters, and richly coffered ceilings recreate the splendor of Renaissance palaces within the confines of the entry vestibule, while elaborate wood carvings in the style of Grinling Gibbons endow paneled interiors with an aristocratic English air. As befits the residence of any self-respecting American industrialist, craftsmanship and technology take on lives of their own. Original elevators glide silently along gleaming rails, secret doors swing back on invisible hinges to reveal walk-in safes, and mammoth ball bearings allow wall-sized pocket doors to disappear with the push of a finger. One senses that their builders intended these houses to last forever, with only regular oiling.

After taking four years to complete his house, George Williams enjoyed

The bannister in the George Williams house is elaborately carved in oak.

The stairwell of the George Williams house is a three-story atrium paneled in wood from top to bottom.

Paneling on the ground floor is decorated with garlands in the style of eighteenth-century English woodcarver Grinling Gibbons.

it for another nine, trading the mansion to newspaper publisher Edward L. Butler in 1908 in exchange for Butler's house down the hill and a large amount of cash. The Butlers' descendants lived at 672 Delaware Avenue until 1976. Charles Williams transferred 690 Delaware Avenue to his daughter Jeannie in 1907 at the time of her marriage to Frederick L. Pratt. During the Depression the City of Buffalo acquired the house in lieu of taxes and converted it into a Civil War memorial. Robert Root's villa was demolished in 1935; the Metcalfs' met a similar fate in 1980, although its stair hall is preserved at the Metropolitan Museum of Art. Buffalo's best corner has lost its residential character as well. Only the houses of Charles and George Williams remain, owned by corporations and occupied, as they were during the tenure of the Williams brothers, by energetic capitalists.

An elaborate order frames the doorway of the drawing room, with the entrance hall and the dining room beyond.

Frederick William Vanderbilt House

# Hyde Park

Hyde Park, New York

1895–99

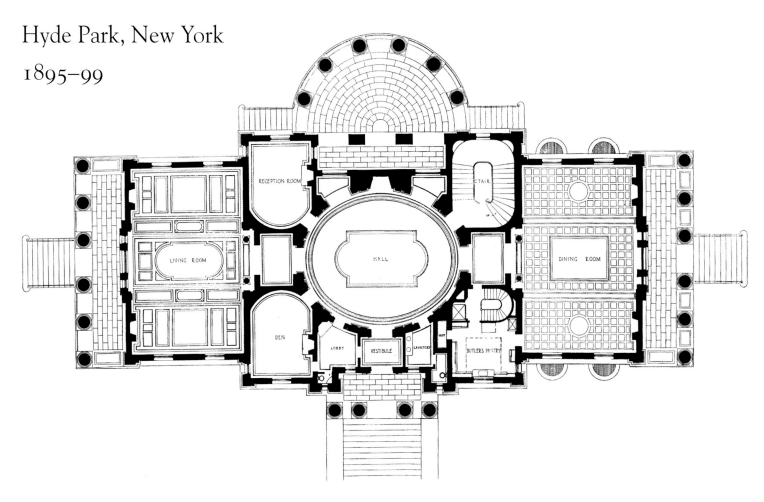

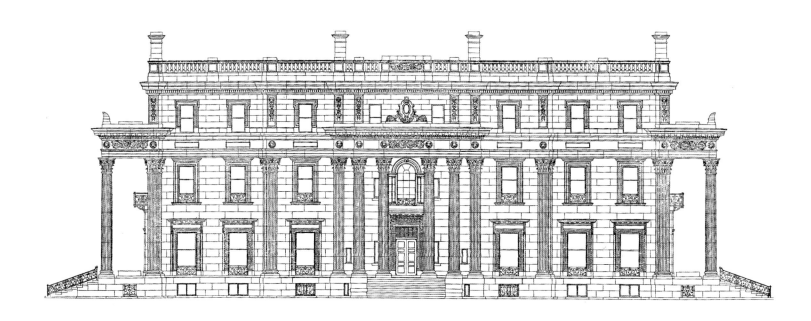

 REDERICK WILLIAM VANDERBILT was the seventh of William Henry Vanderbilt's nine children and the first of Commodore Vanderbilt's descendants to get a college degree. In 1878 he married Louise Anthony Torrance, a divorcée twelve years his senior, an indelicacy that may have upset his father. Frederick inherited only ten million dollars, a legacy belittled by some as a daughter's share of the estate, compared to his older brothers Cornelius and William Kissam who inherited ten times as much. In the 1880s Vanderbilts of that generation had commissioned Richard Morris Hunt to build their impressive array of city and country palaces. For his own Hudson River villa at Hyde Park, Frederick hired McKim, Mead & White.

There is a story that Frederick Vanderbilt first saw Hyde Park from the deck of his yacht en route to visit Ogden Mills at Staatsburgh and that he was so smitten with the abandoned neoclassical villa on the property that he bought it immediately. Records indicate the transfer of ownership from the Langdon estate in May 1895, just as the expansion of Staatsburgh got underway, and it is unclear why Ogden and Elizabeth Mills would have entertained one of America's wealthiest men at an active construction site. Still, the story has a certain resonance given the wealth of the protagonists, the proximity of their country seats, and their choice of the same architect.

Hyde Park was the fifth of seven McKim, Mead & White projects for the Vanderbilts, beginning with stables for the Fifth Avenue Stage Lines and leading to three grand country estates, a town house, an office building, and a mausoleum. The stables were commissioned by Frederick's brother-in-law Elliott Fitch Shepard, for whom the firm designed Woodlea in Scarborough, New York. The mausoleum was erected for another brother-in-law, Hamilton F. Twombley, for whom the firm created Florham in Madison, New Jersey.

Mead and McKim were in charge of the Vanderbilt project with occasional contributions from White. The firm had just finished design drawings for Columbia's Low Library and New York University's Gould Memorial Library, and their performance on the Vanderbilt commission suggests the high level of organization the office had achieved by 1895. The original plan called for a renovation and expansion of the existing villa, along the same lines as the design for Staatsburgh, but when construction got underway it was quickly established that the structure was beyond repair. Assured by their architects that the best features of the older house would be replicated in the new design, the Vanderbilts agreed to start from scratch. The schedule from that point was impressive. In less than eight months the firm

Impressive architecture did not require excessive ornament, as demonstrated by this view of the entry facade and south porch.

In the ground floor plan the ceiling patterns are indicated for the public rooms, and the enormous scale of the house is only revealed by an examination of the smaller spaces. The entrance facade faced east, away from the Hudson River.

The original design banished all gardens and ornamental planting from the vicinity of the house, and the relatively stark landscape emphasizes the view of the Hudson River and the Catskill Mountains in the distance.

programmed, designed, and completed detailed drawings for a project that ultimately cost more than two and a half million dollars. By the time construction was completed in May 1899, McKim, Mead & White's work on the six-hundred-acre estate included a limestone manor and gatehouses, a complex of shingled barns, and a pebbledash-covered pavilion, which was erected in sixty-six working days to provide a temporary residence for the Vanderbilts.

Formal precedents for the main house lie in European neoclassicism filtered through Vanderbilt's nostalgia for the original Langdon mansion and the firm's emerging style for classical villas with two-story porches. The architecture is imperial, with no concession to images of rural domesticity.

A monumental Corinthian order enclosing the principal living floors is set between a low basement and a high attic story. Rectangular porches project from three sides, with a semicircular porch on the river side. All parts are connected to the central block by a continuous base and a deep, plain entablature. The aristocratic expression of restraint extends from the rectangular massing—there are no pediments and no hint of the oval volume that lies within the center of the house—to the austere and widely spaced details. Smooth, plain walls are framed by a system of orthogonal bands, relieved only by bracketed window surrounds and carved medallions, which punctuate rather than obscure the underlying formal structure of the elevations. A few openings are animated with decorative iron balconies, and the roofline is encircled by a stone balustrade. Hidden construction details include steel floor framing, a full complement of bathrooms with hot and cold running water, and underground service from Vanderbilt's electric generator.

The stacking is straightforward: living rooms on the first floor, principal bedrooms on the second floor, and kitchen and service spaces in the basement. The third floor is divided into separate zones for staff and guests, an unusual combination necessitated by the growing popularity of the weekend as a social event and made possible because most of the estate's sixty-six full-time staff lived in the town of Hyde Park. The two main floors are organized around a double-height central oval space crowned by an oculus that brings light into the middle of the house.

The north porch and river facade in the 1890s.

The rooms are grand but highly livable, and the mansion reads as the country retreat of a wealthy, childless couple. The deceptive scale of the interior is the result of skillful space planning and exquisite proportions. An immediate note of welcome is established at the front hall, where twin couches bracketing a large fireplace recall something of the spirit of shingle style living halls. The transformation of the hall into an occupiable room disguises what is in fact a substantial amount of formal circulation. The manipulation of spatial and functional hierarchies is particularly impressive. Public rooms on the first floor are divided into major spaces—drawing room, living hall, and dining room—which are approached and connected axially, and celebrated with ceremonial doorways. Minor spaces, including the den, the reception room, and the staircase, are placed off axis and effectively suppressed behind single-leaf doors. The second floor is dominated by monumental bedrooms, particularly those for Frederick and Louise Vanderbilt, as well as the room for their favorite niece, Margaret Louise Van Alen. Only on the third floor does the enormous size of the house finally reveal itself in winding corridors, innumerable bedrooms, and a full

contingent of support spaces, of which the most intriguing is labeled "Yacht Room" on the original plans.

The Vanderbilts always relied on outside help for decoration. For their New York houses Herter Brothers designed and fabricated furniture, curtains, and fittings. By 1895, however, interior decoration was emerging as an independent profession. At Hyde Park, Ogden Codman, who coauthored *The Decoration of Houses* with Edith Wharton, and George A. Glaenser were responsible for the sitting room, the den, and the principal bedrooms. McKim, Mead & White's decorating hand was originally visible in the drawing room, the dining room with nonmatching twin mantels from White's sources, the halls, and the staircases. The urbanity of the stone and wrought-iron staircase at the first floor is representative of the firm's high-style European interiors. By contrast, the wooden staircase to the third floor with its turned spindles is based on the pulpit in the Sabbatarian Meeting-House, McKim's favorite eighteenth-century Newport room.

Pairs of marble pilasters surround the main hall, fixing the placement of windows, doors, and other elements on major and minor axes.

The house and estate display the work of other architects today. Robert H. Robertson, who created Shelburne for Frederick Vanderbilt's sister Lila Webb, built the coach house and stables in 1897 and converted the structure for automobiles in 1910. In 1905 Vanderbilt wrote to McKim, effectively asking permission to hire Whitney Warren instead of Stanford White to make some changes inside the house. Warren is responsible for the delicately molded balustrade at the second-floor hall and the latticed ceiling above it. Warren, who designed New York's Grand Central Terminal, apologized to McKim for "ruining his design."

In 1940 Margaret Van Alen, the Vanderbilts' niece and heir, donated the estate to the National Park Service. During World War II the entire third floor was used to house security personnel assigned to protect Franklin D. Roosevelt when he was in residence in Hyde Park. Today the Vanderbilt house is open to the public.

Left: Frederick Vanderbilt preferred the intimate scale of the third floor. After his wife died, he moved from an elaborate suite on the second floor to this bedroom.

Right: A corner of the drawing room.

The scale of the interiors can be inferred from the dining room, which has two fireplaces and three exposures. On either side of the window is an orrery, an apparatus invented 1713 by Charles Boyle, 4th Earl of Orrery, to follow the movement of the solar system.

197

# Hermann Oelrichs House

# Rosecliff

## Newport, Rhode Island
## 1897–1902

OSECLIFF, built for Hermann and Tessie Oelrichs, is a masterpiece of formal architecture, created to accommodate a way of life that we can barely imagine today. Theresa Alice Fair Oelrichs was born in Nevada, one of four children of James Graham Fair, a mining engineer, and Theresa Rooney, a hotel operator's daughter. Fair and three partners discovered the Comstock Lode, the country's largest single deposit of silver, which yielded five hundred million dollars' worth of ore before it was depleted in 1898. That fortune was responsible for at least three major commissions for McKim, Mead & White. In addition to Rosecliff, the firm designed a town house at 666 Fifth Avenue (1904–7) for Tessie's sister Virginia, who had married William Kissam Vanderbilt, Jr., and Harbor Hill (1899–1902) in Roslyn, Long Island, for Katherine Duer Mackay, whose father-in-law, John W. Mackay, was one of Fair's original partners.

Even before her marriage Tessie Fair had been the toast of Newport, but as Mrs. Hermann Oelrichs she added a respected lineage to her vast resources, giving her an advantage enjoyed by only a few other hostesses. She consolidated that position through a legendary application of energy, ambition, and organization, assisted initially by a wedding present of one million dollars from her father and, after his death in 1894, a generous inheritance. Rosecliff must be seen as her triumph, as Hermann did not care for Newport. His niece Blanche Oelrichs later wrote that Tessie "was strongly addicted to Society as a business."

If Hermann Oelrichs was described in different terms, it was because he had been presented with different opportunities. Oelrichs was born in Baltimore, the great-grandson of Federalist statesman Harrison Gray Otis. Educated at an elite military academy and in Europe, he apprenticed in his father's shipping business in Bremen and London, returning to New York in 1876. He was the American representative of the North German Lloyd Steamship Company and prospered as the head of Oelrichs & Company, Shipping and Commission Merchants. He was also one of the original

The exterior walls and ornament are constructed of glazed terra-cotta, which White convinced his reluctant client would withstand exposure to the elements.

The facade suggests equal measures of Paris and heaven, an appropriate setting for events such as Tessie Oelrichs's Bal Blanc of 1904.

The asymmetry of the front door location only enriches the delight of Rosecliff's main elevation. The maids' rooms on the third floor are recessed behind the parapet and are generally invisible.

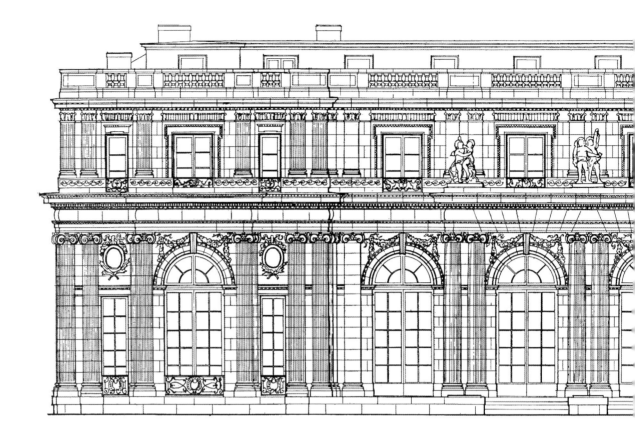

On the ground floor plan the living room is set between two subtly different terraces, connecting the room simultaneously to Bellevue Avenue on one side and the Atlantic Ocean on the other. Hierarchies of family bedrooms and guest quarters are suggested by the second floor plan.

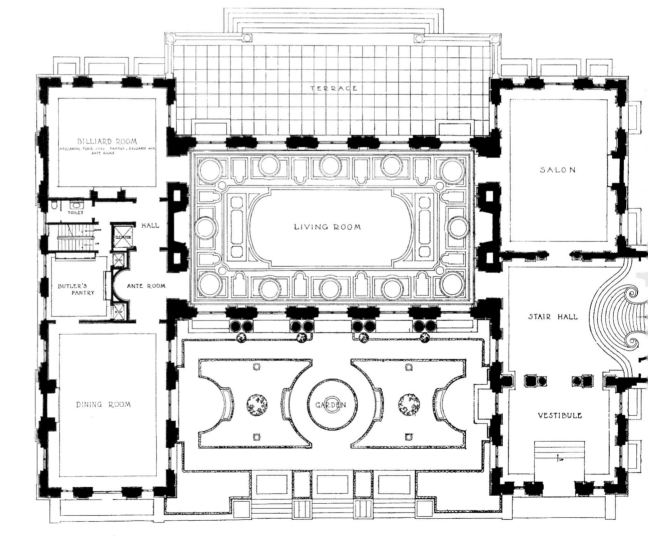

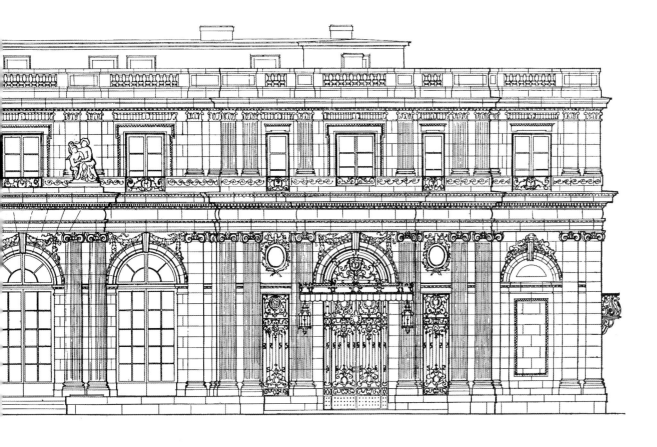

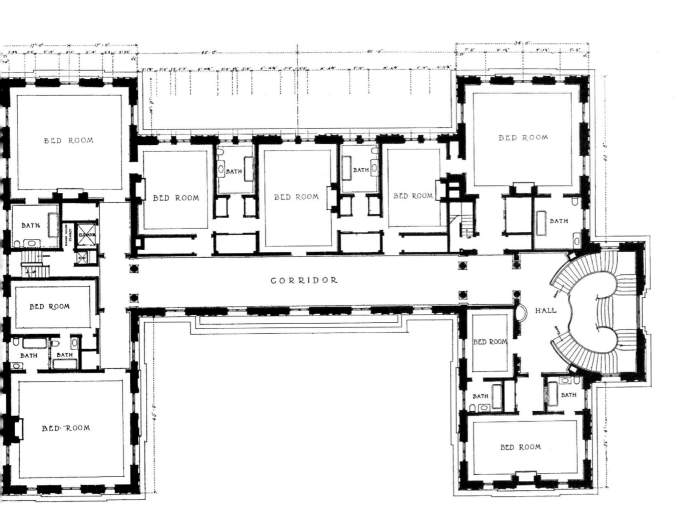

investors, along with Stanford White and David H. King Jr. in the architecturally triumphant and financially troubled Madison Square Garden project. By the time the forty-year-old Oelrichs married Theresa Alice Fair he had
acquired a wide reputation for business acumen, good looks, and athletic
prowess. At his death in 1906 the *New York Times* eulogized him (with a
slight touch of liberal reproach) as "so richly endowed by nature and so perfectly equipped both mentally and physically that his friends have been
almost unanimous in declaring that had he so chosen he might have made
for himself a much higher place in life."

After their marriage in 1890 Mr. and Mrs. Oelrichs lived in New York
at 1 East Fifty-seventh Street and in Newport. In 1891 they bought Rosecliff,
an 1850s frame house on eleven acres overlooking the ocean. Direct access
from Bellevue Avenue was blocked by another property, and Tessie's ambitions for a new house with the right address had to wait until 1897 when
the Oelrichses were able to obtain enough frontage on Bellevue Avenue to
allow a single driveway. The wide open lawn and double driveway seen
today were not completed until 1912, ten years after the house was built,
when more land was acquired.

Stanford White was first consulted in August 1897, probably as soon as
access to Bellevue Avenue became available. Construction began in 1899,
although Tessie was in such a hurry that she began to use the house (artfully
camouflaged) for parties as early as 1900, two years before its completion. Pos-

The descent on the main
staircase was the grandest
moment in Rosecliff's
exquisite choreography.

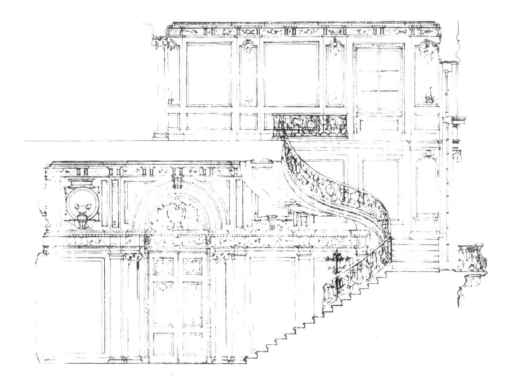

The reception room draws upon the monumental scale of its fireplace, ceiling and chandeliers to corroborate the power of the hostess. Tessie Oelrichs probably greeted guests in this room before they moved into the living room.

sibly she was moved by the spirit of competition with her cousin-in-fortune, Katherine Duer Mackay, whose Harbor Hill was finished the same year.

Hermann Oelrichs moved to San Francisco for the last years of his life. Tessie and their son continued to spend July and August at Rosecliff and the other ten months of the year in Saratoga, Paris, and New York. Hermann Oelrichs Jr. inherited the house from his mother and lived there until 1941. Successive owners included Gertrude Nilsen (1941–43), Ray Alan Van Clief (1943–47), and finally Mr. and Mrs. Edgar J. Monroe (1947–76), who gave the house to the Preservation Society of Newport County. Rosecliff is open to the public as a house museum. There have been almost no changes to its original architecture, save for missing sculpture from the west facade and a 1979–80 program of limited replacement of terra-cotta with concrete. Of the original furnishings, including a white dining room suite, pairs of twisted Spanish columns, and hundreds of pieces of (largely reproduction) French furniture whose enormous scale and rich upholstery made the rooms appear almost modest (one sofa appears to have been over five feet tall), only four jardinieres remain.

The compactness of the house as seen from Bellevue Avenue is deceptive. What appears to be a one-story building is organized around four principal levels: kitchen and service spaces in the cellar, public spaces—entry, reception, living, dining, and billiards—on the ground floor, bedrooms on the second floor, and servants' quarters in the attic.

The plan accommodates a carefully choreographed procession: After passing through the great screened entrance hall, couples would part temporarily. Male guests waited in the hall. Ladies went upstairs to shed their wraps and then made a second and more spectacular entrance via the

A small bronze in the
second floor hall.

voluptuous double-helix staircase. Once rejoined, couples were announced at the door of the reception room and finally deposited in the splendid living room overlooking two terraces at the center of the house. Given the custom of late suppers, miscellaneous social rituals, and simple curiosity, most guests would also enter the dining and billiard rooms, the last spaces in the sequence that started at the front door.

The design of Rosecliff illustrates an aspect of the later work of McKim, Mead & White that, at the time, was called "scientific eclecticism." This term was created to describe buildings that were more or less based on a specific historic prototype—a Renaissance palace, a Roman bath, or an Egyptian temple—selected for its symbolic relevance and manipulated into an appropriate enclosure for a more contemporary program, such as a town house, a train station, or a university library. Jules Hardouin Mansart's Grand Trianon at Versailles was the prototype for Rosecliff, although the palace is barely recognizable after its "scientific" transformation. White retained the spirit and vocabulary of its ornament while he completely transformed the one-story prototype in plan, section, and elevation, inside and out, using new materials such as glazed terra-cotta and new systems such as structural steel frames, electric wiring, and central heating to create a modern building in a wholly original design. The final effect has an agreeably traditional air, and for this quality alone the building is sometimes criticized as slavishly derivative.

As with all of McKim, Mead & White's later houses, Rosecliff is both diagrammatic and complex, but its impact is undeniable. By day the composition reads as a simple collage in three colors: blue for sky and water, green for earth and trees, and white for man-made interventions. Close up, the enrichment of the facades with putti, garlands, and musical instruments makes the terra-cotta look as if it had been formed out of the clouds and whitecaps surrounding the site. By night the lighted interiors would have been visible through shirred white casements, making the building appear as a giant illuminated jewel box.

Its perfection in proportion, scale, and ornament, as well as its effortless accommodation of the choreography of an Olympian social life, is made more interesting by the tension between symmetry and asymmetry that runs through the design. Like all of the firm's grand houses designed after 1885, Rosecliff appears symmetrical. But it does not cleave to the tradition of a centrally placed front door, a characteristic usually considered so essential that most of the design interest in large houses arises out of the gymnastics required to achieve it. The placement of the front door in the south

The ornament of the dining room implies entertainment, while its proportions suggest power.

wing reflects the natural circulation diagram and allows the house to be planned around its processional requirements as well as its most important room. The original problem of access to Bellevue Avenue, which placed the driveway tight against the southern edge of the property, may also have encouraged the architects to proceed with such an unusual door location.

Even discounting the off-center door, neither the massing nor the elevations are perfectly symmetrical. The robust ornamental scheme of the elevations allows small entresol windows to peek out almost unnoticed through openings in squinches and spandrels. The bay enclosing the great stair and its exceptionally placed landing window are celebrated with a romantic balcony isolated above the rose garden. The north facade with its sunken kitchen court reveals the full complexity of the service spaces required to support the operations of a large country house. A subtle foil to Rosecliff's public face, the north elevation shows that art can accommodate mechanics, and that a classical vocabulary can be relevant in the industrial age.

# Robert W. Patterson House

Washington, D.C.    1900–1903

HEN ROBERT WILSON PATTERSON's father-in-law, Joseph Medill, died in 1899, Patterson became editor-in-chief of Medill's newspapers, including the *Chicago Tribune*, and his ability to realize his ambition as an architectural patron advanced to a new level. He and his wife, Elinor, immediately began planning a Washington residence in 1900 to take advantage of Robert's elevated status and the capital's winter social season.

The Pattersons were experienced clients. In *McKim, Mead & White Architects*, Leland Roth comments that the interior of their Chicago town house by McKim, Mead & White was "not as grand as the exterior might suggest." The Pattersons must have felt the same way. They informed their architects that for the Washington house they required grand interiors, suitable for entertaining on a large scale. The firm complied, designing a private house with rooms of an almost public scale and at the same time producing a building of uncommon generosity towards its urban context. White himself described the design as possessing a "light and rather joyous character." The Patterson commission marked the beginning of the firm's intense involvement with the nation's capital, which at its peak in 1902 included the enlargement of the White House, a new campus for the Army War College, and membership on the Senate Park Commission to develop guidelines for the restitution of the Mall and the rehabilitation of L'Enfant's 1791 plan for the city's public core.

The Patterson house overlooks Dupont Circle at the oblique intersection of two major streets, creating an irregular lot with two unequal frontages. McKim, Mead & White was familiar with the Washington grid through a series of previous residential and commercial commissions, from an unbuilt 1882 design for David H. King Jr. to large corner town houses for Thomas Nelson Page in 1896–97 and for Admiral Thomas O. Selfridge in 1897–99. The partners must have felt a particular sympathy for the Washington grid with its Beaux-Arts vistas. The Patterson house represented another opportunity to employ L'Enfant's imperial geometry in the creation of a distinguished, site-specific design in a highly visible location.

The house practically turns Dupont Circle's vast interior park into a private front yard. Its butterfly scheme, with a shortened forecourt embraced by equal wings, treats the two frontages impartially to establish a third, more major axis, reducing the intersection of two broad streets to an extension of the forecourt and establishing an almost proprietary relationship to the park beyond. The geometry of the scheme is extremely sophis-

Preceding pages:
The symmetrical arrangement of the facade around a recessed forecourt conceals a dynamic system of movement and spaces within, recalling the plan and effect of E. D. Morgan's Beacon Rock.

The exterior walls and ornament are principally glazed terra-cotta. Only the columns and the panels between the windows are marble.

ticated. Exterior symmetry is achieved on the street facades with the difference in frontages taken up by an irregular side yard. The indented forecourt reduces the interior volume (and the dimensions of the public rooms) in favor of a gesture toward the public right-of-way, giving the building its distinctly aristocratic bearing on the street. In his monograph on the firm, Richard Guy Wilson cites correspondence between White and the Pattersons in which the architects had to fight for their scheme, resorting at one point to the disingenuous argument that the forecourt would "save some money on the cost of the house."

The general character and ornament of the exterior evokes Italian Renaissance prototypes without suggesting any single model. It also hints at the reincarnation of the "White City," the buildings of the 1893 World's Columbian Exposition in Chicago, which signaled the firm's shift toward an exclusively classical vocabulary. McKim, Mead & White's vision of the appropriate architecture for the city of the American Renaissance sits naturally on Dupont Circle, anticipating a similar expression in Washington's public architecture over the next fifty years and explaining the powerful influence that McKim would have over his peers on the Senate Park Commission. The white walls of the Patterson house, decorated with specific details such as Ionic orders, attic story, enriched bands, and garlanded window pediments particularly recall the firm's New York State Building, which the Pattersons must have seen at the fair and may have admired.

The planning of the house places secondary reception rooms on the ground floor, along with a large entry hall, a broad staircase, and Washington's first attached garage. The three major public spaces—dining room, library, and ballroom—open off a large central hall on the second floor, with a ducal balcony overlooking the forecourt. It is clear that the designers labored over the plan, for the manipulations required to achieve exterior symmetry make the arrangement of the second floor appear deceptively simple. Service spaces fill in the rear of the site, while the transition to the regular geometry of the front rooms is achieved through a balanced but completely asymmetrical composition incorporating the stairs, balcony, and ballroom doors. The third floor contains the family bedrooms with guest rooms located half a floor above, a civilized separation that gives everyone a measure of privacy, retains the design's compact circulation, and creates additional ceiling height in the ballroom.

In keeping with its practice in the later, more formal houses, McKim, Mead & White hired outside decorators to develop and execute the firm's designs for the elaborate interiors. Wilson assigns the ballroom and ground-

The system of ornament reinforces the structure of the elevations. Enrichment of window frames, wall panels, building corners, and floor levels establishes the rhythm of the facades along the street and emphasizes important openings. The butterfly plan of the house allows for views of the exterior elevations from within.

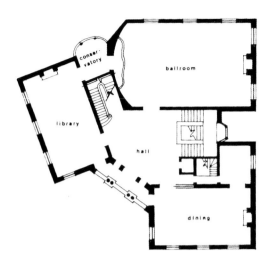

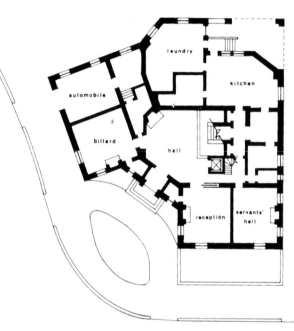

Second floor plan and
ground floor plan.

The planning characteristics
of the firm's early living
halls are retained in the
fireplace and stairs, as
is the welcoming spirit and
the easy flow of space.
The fireplace at the corner
of the front hall acts like
a mirror, off which the
main interior axis of the
stairs ricochets toward
the front door.

The Pattersons' ballroom (opposite) and dining room (above) must have been heavily used during the Washington social season, which took place during the winter while Congress was in session. Dupont Circle was known as the Winter Newport.

floor reception room to Allard & Fils, who also worked on Rosecliff and the Mills house, the library to Marcotte & Company, the dining room to Tiffany Studios, and the halls and the conservatory that originally linked the library and the ballroom to Hayden and Company.

The Patterson family owned 15 Dupont Circle until 1949, lending it to President and Mrs. Coolidge in 1927 while the White House was being renovated. Charles Lindbergh was the Coolidges' guest during the ceremonies that marked his triumphal return from Paris that June. After Mrs. Patterson's death the house was occupied by their daughter Cissy Patterson, who left it to the Red Cross. The Washington Club bought the building in 1951 and continues to use it in the most sympathetic way, employing its still grand rooms for entertaining on a large scale and even tracking down much of the original furniture. Minor changes to the original design include a 1956 wing accommodating a kitchen and banquet room, the enclosure of the stairs above the second floor, and the elimination of the conservatory.

# Joseph Pulitzer House

New York

1900–1903

OSEPH PULITZER, owner of the *St. Louis Post Dispatch* and the *New York World,* was a longstanding client of McKim, Mead & White in spite of the publisher's legendary irascibility. He retained the architects in 1891 and again in 1894 to modify his house at 10 East Fifty-fifth Street, which they had originally designed in 1882 for Charles T. Barney. In 1895 he hired them to expand his cottage in Bar Harbor, Maine. The town house and all its contents, including Pulitzer's library, were destroyed by fire in January 1900. Nine months later he directed his architects to design a replacement to be built on a triple lot on East Seventy-third Street off Fifth Avenue.

Pulitzer suffered from weak eyesight and poor health throughout his life. By 1900 he was nearly blind, and the facade design had to be presented as a series of architectural models. He rejected McKim, Mead & White's two initial schemes. Possibly the French Renaissance chateau with which they had recently satisfied Katherine Mackay and the Florentine palazzo they built for Robert Wilson Patterson lacked sufficient plasticity to interest a client who could touch but could no longer see. McKim, Mead & White then turned to Baldassare Longhena, the architect of the high Venetian baroque, for their third submission. They proposed a Venetian palace combining the superimposed orders and rhythms of Longhena's Palazzo Pesaro with his canal entrance to the C'a Rezzonico. Pulitzer's fingertips must have appreciated the Venetian's tactile formula, which consisted of unbroken rustication at the ground floor, liberal use of columns and arches in the upper stories, and virtual elimination of wall surfaces.

The completed facade, which would look perfectly natural in Venice, is startling in New York, even after the gritty texture of Longhena's original was watered down for American consumption. The synthesis is striking in its boldness, both in relation to the firm's other designs as well as in juxtaposition with the building's more conventional neighbors. The Pulitzer mansion is aristocratic and foreign, particularly in the return of the street facade for the full depth of the western elevation, suggesting a power that transcended the law of party walls. The building's impact at street level is undeniable as well, no more so than where its relentless banding consumes even the columns at the front door. Pedestrians can also appreciate its lessons on the proper superimposition of orders, with a smooth Doric base supporting an Ionic piano nobile. Sadly, the exquisite Corinthian order at the top, intended to be seen at a distance, is obscured by Manhattan's narrow side streets.

The black iron gates disappear against the light stone to create a monumental void at the entrance.

Seventy-third Street elevation.

Entrance hall and stairwell.

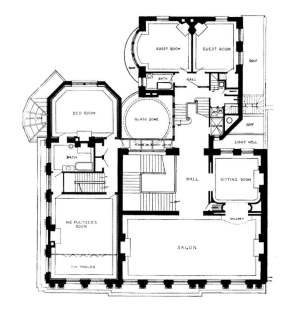

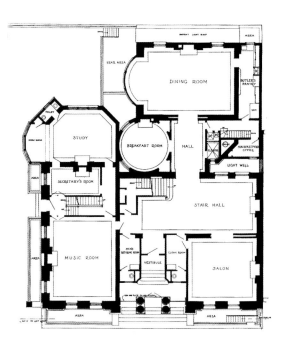

By all accounts, the process of designing the interiors was sheer tor-
ture, exasperating even the normally patient Mead. Pulitzer, who had not
wanted to pay for the preliminary schemes, was both peremptory and inde-
cisive. After cautioning his architects that he would accept "no ballroom,
music room, or picture gallery under any disguise," he extended the ban to
French furniture, insisting that he wanted an "American" house. The paneling in the front hall was probably fabricated in New York by Herter Brothers, but the elegant trompe l'oeil boiserie in the remarkably ballroom-like
salon came from Allard's Parisian workshops. There was plenty of room on

The original ground
floor plan reveals the
organization of the house
into acoustically separate
precincts. Finding even this
arrangement inadequate,
Pulitzer eventually built his
bedroom in the rear yard.

the seventy-five foot lot for representations of all cultures. The final design included approximately fifty separate spaces above grade, ranging from an organ loft overlooking the grand staircase to a squash court, presumably for Pulitzer's children.

With evidence of so much activity programmed into the house, it would be easy to forget that Pulitzer's most significant infirmity was his intolerance of sound of any kind. His architects were required to develop a design that isolated Pulitzer's personal quarters from household noises. Not surprisingly, the final plan is unlike anything else the architects produced. They grouped related rooms on each floor into three separate blocks, each enclosed in thick masonry walls, with floors separated by soundproof construction. Pulitzer's wing on the west side of the lot was padded from floor to ceiling, and the wing itself so isolated from the rest of the house that his access to the public zone was limited to a bridge crossing over the skylit circular breakfast room, plus a private staircase that led directly to the proscribed music room.

Ultimately the architects failed to make the house completely sound-proof, and no efforts succeeded in eliminating the noise of one particular

The salon on the piano nobile was executed by Allard in Paris to McKim, Mead & White's design. The frame surrounding the mirror over the mantle creates a forced perspective, a device from Italian baroque architecture.

A bridge within the glazed skylight over the original breakfast room connected Joseph Pulitzer's apartment to the family quarters. (Collection of The New-York Historical Society)

pump to Pulitzer's satisfaction. In 1904 he hired Foster, Gade & Graham to design an even more isolated bedroom at the rear of the house, closing off the rear garden. Supported on ball bearings and isolated by double acoustical doors, the addition finally provided the eccentric publisher with a good night's sleep.

Not surprisingly, the owner's idiosyncratic requirements did not translate into a generic dream house. Following Pulitzer's death in 1911, his family moved out of 7 East Seventy-third Street while retaining ownership, possibly because no one wanted to buy it. The building had been shuttered and abandoned for two decades when *New Yorker* writer James Thurber paid a visit in 1934. He marveled at its forlorn condition and vast size— "cold, lonely, and sad, but still magnificent, and a touch mysterious, the mansion is like a grand duchess gone blind and deaf in her old age." Shortly thereafter the building was converted into a multiple dwelling, with each unit surrounded by heavy masonry demising walls and separated by plenty of acoustical insulation. Today 7 East Seventy-third Street is a fashionable cooperative apartment building, saved because the very features installed to accommodate the exceptional paranoia of the head of one household made the structure an ideal candidate to accommodate an additional fourteen.

Today the breakfast room is a separate apartment, and the skylight is filled in.

# Payne Whitney and Henry Cook Houses

## New York

## 1902–7

HEN PAYNE WHITNEY married Helen Hay in 1902, Oliver Payne's wedding present was a mansion on Fifth Avenue. Stanford White, on whose advice Colonel Payne relied for matters ranging from bidding on art at auction to landscape improvements for his Georgia plantation, would be the architect. Payne Whitney, the financier's favorite nephew and namesake, had been a champion oarsman at Yale and for the rest of his life would be described as a sportsman. He was the son of William C. Whitney, Secretary of the Navy under Cleveland, who was better known for controlling most of New York's streetcar lines and for whom the firm had substantially renovated an estate on Long Island and two

The public face of the Whitney house was realized in three varieties of white stone: pure white statuary marble for the front door (left), strongly veined marble for the entrance hall (opposite), and Vermont granite for the exterior walls and details (opposite, above).

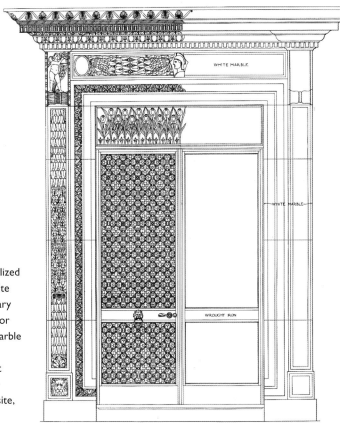

houses on Fifth Avenue. The Hays were the Whitneys' peers in all respects. Helen Hay was an accomplished poet. Her father John Hay was the Secretary of State under McKinley and Roosevelt, and she had grown up in one half of a double town house by Richardson. Prior to attending the wedding himself, White directed Tiffany's to send a cast of Saint-Gaudens's *Diana* to Miss Helen Hay at her father's house in Washington.

The merger of two families of this stature demanded the best possible address, a requirement that introduced Henry Cook into the equation. Cook, a Manhattan land speculator, owned an entire city block at Fifth Avenue and Seventy-ninth Street, which he was selling off in high-priced lots to Phippses, Mortimers, and Fishes. Acting as a one-man zoning board, Cook prohibited any development that included such offensive components as stables, commerce, or even behavior that did not meet his exacting standards. After he sold Oliver Payne the mid-block lot at 972 Fifth Avenue, Cook elected to build a house for himself on the remaining Fifth Avenue parcel, hiring Payne's contractor, the J. C. Lyons Building & Operating Company, as well as Payne's architect. Cook also reserved a third lot as a service alley, permitting direct access from Seventy-ninth Street to the basement kitchens at the rear of each house.

The multiple layers of the
Whitneys' entrance hall
reverse the natural relationship of interior and exterior
space: the marble paneled
perimeter frames a monu-
mental fireplace, stairs, and
doors to individual rooms.
The circular colonnade at
the center supports a
shallow dome decorated
with lattice and vines. The
sculpture, acquired by
White as a Roman antiquity,
is now thought to be an
early work by Michelangelo.

227

Detail of a plaster relief panel in the ceiling of the Whitneys' entrance hall.

Stanford White designed a unified facade for the two separate houses, rendered entirely in white Vermont granite. He wrapped the walls with five stories of superimposed orders, built up from a simple classical vocabulary of smooth rustication, double pilasters, and deeply projecting string courses, accented with Renaissance motifs ranging from wave moldings to lion heads. The Whitneys' curved, forty-five foot front carries three bays along Fifth Avenue, with an additional seven needed for the wall overlooking the garden. Cook's house only required two additional bays of granite cladding to complete the effect of a double town house.

White used the Whitneys' house to explore the decorative potential of his subdued order. The facade of 972 Fifth Avenue is enriched with Wedgwood-like reliefs, swagged panels, and winged putti crammed into the spandrels of the arches. The front door, a grille of iron leaves with gold accents, is surrounded by a white marble frame carved in a delicate, high Renaissance style relief. The final effect is one of welcome, consistent with the building's high exposure to the street. By comparison, the more private nature of Cook's program is suggested by its plainer facade and by details

The Whitneys' reception room, called the Venetian Room by Helen Hay Whitney, is executed in antique mirror with gilded moldings. The cornice is a coved trellis of porcelain flowers.

such as the lion heads guarding his massive wooden front doors. In spite of White's admiration of the cinquecento, there is something rather Victorian about the elevations. The regular rhythm of stacked floors and crisp articulation of individual components suggest the industrial revolution more than the Renaissance, while the plate glass double-hung sash and the high ratio of window to wall evoke latitudes further north than Italy.

At 22,000 square feet, 972 Fifth Avenue was big enough to accommodate White's imagination as well as the public and private life of one of America's richest families. The main stair connects the entry to the piano nobile, with a separate stair leading up from the third floor to family quarters, servants' rooms, and a vaulted fifth-floor studio for Mrs. Whitney that one 1910 observer considered the best room in the house. Almost all rooms have a southern exposure on the garden facade, although the garden itself was part of the property next door.

The Whitney interiors reveal Stanford White at maximum volume as a decorator, demonstrating equal measures of taste, imagination and resources. In collaboration with the Whitneys, White extended Payne's generosity so

Detail of the ceiling in Henry Cook's study.

In the Cooks' drawing room, relatively flat paneling, a small mantle, and a delicately incised cornice exaggerate the dramatic vertical scale of the walls.

Henry Cook's study was realized with medieval fittings, creating the atmosphere of an Edwardian male retreat.

far that the architect was afraid to reveal the full cost of the project to its benefactor until it was too late to retreat. The level of extreme luxury is established at the circular entrance hall, framed by eight marble columns surrounding a marble fountain that White assembled out of fragments of older pieces. The ceiling is a shallow plaster dome, molded into a lattice pattern and embellished with reliefs of polychromed cherubs illustrating themes of Eros and Amour, an appropriate choice for a wedding present. The semi-outdoor quality of the white stone hall contrasts with the jewel-like detail and abundant gilding of the adjacent mirrored reception room, one of White's most original creations, and the subdued comfort of Mr. Whitney's leather paneled office beyond. The cool marble walls of the main stairs were similarly relieved by four life-size allegorical figures of the seasons in stained glass by John La Farge and the elaborate woodwork on the ceiling and doors of the second floor hall.

Stanford White filled the rooms with the treasures of a European shopping trip that he conducted for the Whitneys in the summer of 1905. Period photographs testify to White's connections with the architectural salvage market as well as his fearlessness in juxtaposing rich elements such as brocade-lined walls, ceilings from Spanish and Italian palaces, painted friezes, pagan sculpture, and religious images. When he could not find an authentic antique, he created a new one. Even with established sources and a willing client it took time to spend a million dollars, the reported cost of the house and its furnishings. While the design was in place by 1902, the house was not quite finished in the fall of 1906 when the impatient couple moved in. White did not live to see all the rooms completed, and both of Helen Hay Whitney's children were born before she ever spent a night in 972 Fifth Avenue.

Cook's house is simpler inside, but only by comparison with the Whitneys'. Organized around an elegant five-story elliptical staircase, its major rooms are set at the front and the very back, with service spaces overlooking the light well shared by the two houses. Cook's bedroom and study were on the third floor; his daughter had a similar arrangement on the fourth. The floors of 972 and 973 align, and, with its narrower frontage, Cook's house has smaller rooms with exceptional proportions. The second floor drawing room of 973 sets off its eighteen foot-high walls with painted wood paneling, tall mirrors and a low, flush mantle. Fabricated by Allard & Fils to White's design, it is one of the rare spaces that replicates the dramatic vertical exaggeration of the Louis XVI style.

The Whitneys owned 972 Fifth Avenue until 1949; since 1952 it has been the Cultural Services division of the French Embassy. Cook died before

The gentle swell of the bow front of the Whitney house contrasts with the projecting base and second-floor entablature of the Cook facade.

his house was finished; Payne Whitney bought it from his estate, finished construction, and allowed Cook's daughter to remain until after World War I. The Whitneys used the smaller building as a guest house and as a bachelor residence for their son Jock, selling it in 1949 as well. For a short period Henry Cook's house was used by an institution before reverting to private ownership, and today it is one of the last Fifth Avenue mansions still occupied as a single-family residence.

# Percy Rivington Pyne House

New York

1906–12

ERCY PYNE'S neo-federalist town house at 680 Park Avenue bears witness to the entire history of McKim, Mead & White, both in its stylish architecture and in its multiple associations between client and architect. Pyne, a financier and philanthropist, was the grandson of Moses Taylor, founder of the National City Bank and an investor in the Atlantic Cable. Taylor's 1876 commission for a summer house in Elberon, New Jersey, had confirmed the young McKim's professional credentials within that seaside colony, and the design of its monumental gables demonstrated the power of his reductive architecture. Taylor's two sons became clients of the firm; the elder, H. A. C. Taylor, commissioned one of the most significant of their Newport houses. A continuous chain of commissions ranging from McKim, Mead & White's masterful 1880 shingle style house in Elberon for Victor Newcomb to their 1904 adaptive reuse of Ithiel Town's Custom House for the National City Bank establishes Moses Taylor as a vital progenitor of the firm's success.

Pyne's site at the top of a hill on the northwest corner of Park Avenue and East Sixty-eighth Street had not always been so desirable. Park Avenue was once Fourth Avenue, where smoke-belching locomotives ran through an open pit en route to Grand Central Terminal at Forty-second Street. With the conversion of the locomotives to electric power and the enclosure of the viaduct in the early 1900s, the area was transformed from a shanty town

On the balance of the elevations, ornamental enrichment is limited to a few choice details such as ironwork at the balconies and the string course separating the marble base from the brick upper stories.

The elevations of the Percy Pyne house rely on perfect proportions and elegant details rather than upon dramatic architectural gestures. The density of ornament was significantly increased around the entrance.

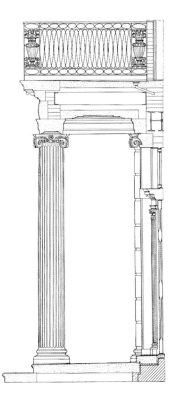

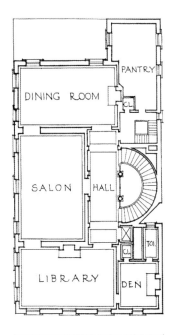

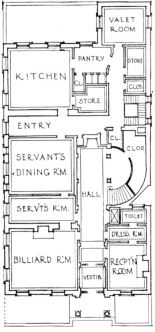

Second floor plan and
ground floor plan.

into one of the major achievements of the City Beautiful movement. Pyne was not the first society figure to build a town house on Park Avenue, but his decision confirmed its metamorphosis into New York's fashionable boulevard.

By the time Pyne contacted McKim, Mead & White in January 1906, McKim was heavily involved with institutional commissions and White was the firm's premier house designer. Whether Pyne wanted a house by his grandfather's old friend or one by his brilliant partner is moot, for six months later White was dead and McKim's health was beginning to fail. Pyne's project was put on hold for four years, and not until 1910 did construction finally get underway. In the interim, design control at McKim, Mead & White had come firmly into the possession of William Mitchell Kendall, McKim's principal assistant and leader of the second generation of partners. Kendall is best remembered for the inspired paraphrase of Herodotus— "Neither snow nor rain, nor heat, nor gloom of night stays these couriers from the swift completion of their appointed rounds"—with which he completed the firm's competition entry for the Post Office on Eighth Avenue. He had been with the office since 1882 when it was designing exuberant shingle style cottages, but as McKim's alter ego, Kendall was committed to the more disciplined traditions of Greece and Rome. He also inherited McKim's appreciation for early American architecture.

In their decision to design 680 Park Avenue as a revival of the federal period town house, McKim, Mead & White continued one of their most picturesque and durable contributions to the American city. Colonial New England's ethos of culture and discipline is represented in the combination of smooth red brick walls laid up with hairline mortar joints; chaste marble trim with a discreet display of elegant classical details; tall, multipaned, double-hung sashes with thin mullions; and balconies, fences, and grilles straight out of London architect L. N. Cottingham's *The Ornamental Metal-Workers Directory* of 1823. The genesis of that style within the firm's portfolio probably lies in the houses designed in the late 1880s along Boston's Commonwealth Avenue, but the evident delight with which the partners applied its remarkably adaptable formula can be traced to their early appreciation for the architecture of Salem and Portsmouth. Facades in the federal style appear with some regularity after the mid-1890s in designs such as their Washington, D.C., residence for Thomas Nelson Page and New York town houses for James Junius Goodwin, Phillip A. Rollins, and Charles Dana Gibson. The first American ancestor of the Pyne house is Charles Bulfinch's third Harrison Gray Otis house completed in 1808, a connection that no architect would be ashamed to acknowledge.

Credit for the details of Pyne's federal style elevations must be assigned to Kendall. He was responsible for its lightly rusticated limestone base, flemish-bond brick walls and blind arches, and spirited but restrained play of lintels, enframements, and console brackets. He could also claim credit for the delicate details of its entrance porch, enhanced by the single blind marble arch above, and the wholly rhetorical but absolutely essential combination of segmental-arched broken pediment, lacy balcony, and relief panels that brings the south elevation to a subdued crescendo along the side street. Kendall was able to extend the basic vocabulary of his facades north along Park Avenue in 1926 when he replaced the Pynes' garden with a house for their son-in-law Oliver D. Filley. The three successive architects who built adjoining houses saw no reason to abandon the formula, and the Pyne-Davison row on Park Avenue is still the most coherent neo-federal block in New York.

The Pyne interiors combine skillful planning with pure neoclassical design. A semicircular stair enriched with ascending orders sweeps from the marble entrance hall to the third floor under the eye of an exquisitely divided laylight. The first floor contains small reception and service rooms; the main public rooms are all on the piano nobile. The formal library, dining,

Pyne's library was an opportunity for Kendall to indulge his fondness for shallow vaults. He would later design serenely arched bridges in Cambridge, Massachusetts and Washington, D. C.

The breakfast room on the third floor allowed the family to dine upstairs The French wallpaper, designed by A. Leroy of Paris in 1832, depicts Pizarro's conquests in South America.

The ceiling of the drawing room contains small paintings inset in elaborate plaster tracery. In Robert Adam's eighteenth-century originals, the geometry of the ceiling would have been repeated in the carpet.

and drawing rooms display the range of neoclassical interiors, with the Adam ceiling of the drawing room holding pride of place. The transition from public to private occurs at the third floor, which contained the master and principal guest bedrooms as well as an elegant family breakfast room. From there a smaller flight of stairs rises to the fourth floor where Pyne's five children slept, and to the fifth floor where the servants lived. A career in domestic service to Percy Pyne offered more that just a view of Park Avenue. He retired old employees with pensions, a philanthropy that was sufficiently novel to warrant inclusion in his *New York Times* obituary.

Pyne died in August 1929, untroubled by harbingers of the Depression. His wife continued to occupy the house until 1947 when, after refusing an offer from the Stalin government, she sold it to the Chinese, who immediately resold it to the Russians. The Soviet Mission to the United Nations occupied 680 Park Avenue until 1965, most memorably on September 21, 1960, when Soviet Premier Khrushchev harangued the press from the balcony of Kendall's civilized entrance porch. In 1965 the Marquesa deCuevas, a daughter of John D. Rockefeller Jr., saved the house and its two neighbors from the wrecker's ball, donating the Pyne house to the predecessor of the Americas Society, Inc., the current owners. The 1965 renovation and restoration of 680 Park Avenue was completed by Walker O. Cain and Thomas Moore, who as Walker O. Cain & Associates represented the direct successors and were the last formal connection to the original partnership of Charles Follen McKim, William Rutherford Mead, and Stanford White.

The main staircase, which runs from the first to the third floors, illustrates a high level of control in its planning, design, and execution.

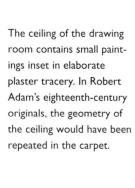

James L. Breese House

# The Orchard

Southampton, Long Island

1898–1900; addition, 1906

T IS EASY TO SEE WHY Jimmy Breese was a friend of Stanford White's. Their mutual avocations included hunting, fishing, and automobile racing. In a 1905 letter to his wife, White describes a Florida automobile race in which he and Breese drove ten miles in nine minutes: "as near flying, I think, as I will ever get in my life." Other shared interests maintained that pace, including Breese's alternate career as a photographer and memberships ranging from Canada's clean-living Ristigouche River Salmon Club to New York's less savory Sewer Club. A seat on the New York Stock Exchange, supported by a substantial amount of inherited wealth, allowed Breese to list his occupation as financier while engaging in other, more indulgent enterprises, not the least of which was architectural patronage.

In 1895 Breese acquired a thirty-acre tract of land in Southampton, which included a working farm and an early-nineteenth-century ship captain's house. In 1898 he commissioned McKim, Mead & White to move, enlarge, and transform the older structure into a villa of a scale and image appropriate to an American gentleman's estate. By this time, though, the firm was sufficiently large and successful that the partners might easily have declined a commission with such restrictive constraints. But Breese was a friend of the firm, and the project must have appealed to the architects who had been dealing with similar issues at White's country house, Box Hill, since 1884, and on far less capital.

McKim is generally credited with the exterior, White with the interior. They expanded the original house through a strategy of flanking pavilions connected by hyphens, extending the facade over two hundred fifty feet from east to west. The articulated links preserve the domestic scale of the composition and allow a little freedom from the restrictive planning dimensions of the older structure. A second addition was completed in 1906 when the east pavilion was transformed from a double-height rustic

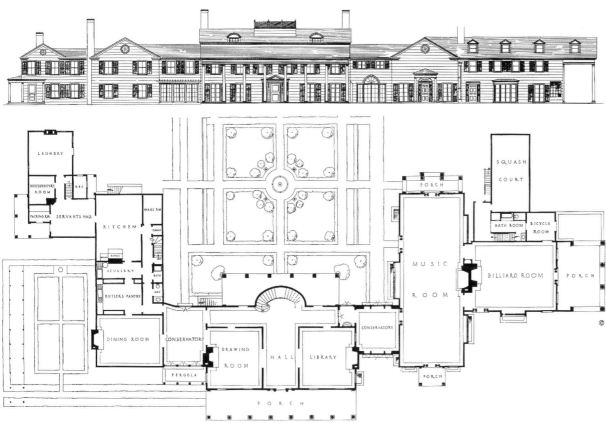

Above: Like Ogden Mills's Staatsburgh and White's own Box Hill, the original cottage is still visible at the heart of a substantially enlarged structure.

Left: The distribution of the program among small-scaled pavilions is evident in the ground floor plan and entrance elevation.

The Palladian window at the rear of the house overlooks the formal walled garden. Urns of flowers originally sat on the porch roof over each of the columns.

studio, whose rubble fireplace had been constructed from the foundation stones of the original house, into the present music room.

Olmsted worked on the landscaping. The grounds around the house consist mostly of long stretches of open lawn punctuated by ancient trees and thick hedges. The walled orchard is the principal built element of the formal landscape design. Inside the long oblong of the orchard garden the perimeter is defined by stucco columns and whitewashed walls of clinker brick supporting a pergola originally fashioned from gnarled tree branches. The columns are on white marble bases set flush in the herringbone brick paving. A fountain once featured a marble infant carved by White's friend, sculptor Janet Scudder.

The exterior architecture is a medley of American themes, in which patriotic and historic references abound. The composition of articulated, hierarchical, and balanced masses is that of a Palladian manor out of *Vitruvius Britannicus* via northern Virginia, while the individual units replicate the eighteenth-century farmhouses that defined Southampton's landscape well into the twentieth century. The design simultaneously quotes Washington and Jefferson. The original captain's cottage is subsumed behind a

A two-story gabled porch dominates the east end of the house.

monumental entrance porch à la Mount Vernon, and the giant order superimposed over the multiple stories at the east end recalls a similar organiz-
ing device on the Virginia state capitol. The bombé curve enclosing the
new circular staircase at the rear of the house evokes the architecture of
Bulfinch and the federalist period, and the stained-glass windows in the
music room reproduce the coats of arms of the original signers of the Dec-
laration of Independence.

The exterior details also manage to transcend their more identifiable
references to illustrate the firm's deep familiarity with the roots of American
architecture, leading back to England and Rome. The eighteenth-century
New England of the Unitarians and tea traders is seen through the repeated
use of white painted wood walls, simple pedimented gables, low shingled
roofs, louvered shutters, and round-headed dormers, although one looks in

The relatively low ceiling
height of the old farmhouse
transforms McKim, Mead &
White's neoclassical
medallion into an integral
component of the door
surround.

vain for the scallop-shell motif that appeared throughout their early work. The large panes of glass in the one-over-one windows create deep shadows that are more Vitruvian than colonial. The entire composition is wrapped in thirty-seven-inch cypress shakes with a fourteen-inch exposure, a treatment that imparts a monumental scale to the elevations and is without precedent in the firm's work.

Most public rooms have relatively simple colonial detailing with a few rich details, such as the large plaster medallion on the entry hall ceiling. This simplicity works well with the low ceiling heights and the unusual internal planning imposed by the original house, and it gives the interiors

a distinctly American feel. By contrast, the 1906 addition is unabashedly imperial. White assembled individual Renaissance stone carvings to create a monumental mantle, combined medieval linenfold paneling with a gilded and coffered wood ceiling, and installed a pipe organ, played from a console decorated with Jacobean strapwork.

In 1935 Breese sold the house to Charles E. Merrill, who converted the squash court into an exquisite art deco dining room and left the property to Amherst College at his death in 1956. The Nyack School for Boys occupied the site from 1960, abandoning it to the tax rolls in 1972. In 1980, Whitefields Associates and the Planning Appeals Board of the Village of Southampton negotiated a zoning change that allowed the creation of twenty-nine condominium units in exchange for preserving the property. Simon Thorensen & Associates were the architects for the subdivision of the main house itself into five units.

Today the music room is
used for grand receptions.

The water tower at
Box Hill, Stanford White's
summer house in
St. James, Long Island.

# Selected Bibliography

Andrews, Wayne. *Architecture, Ambition, & Americans: A Social History of American Architecture.* New York: The Free Press, 1947, 1964.

Baker, Paul R. *Stanny: The Gilded Life of Stanford White.* New York: The Free Press, 1989.

Baldwin, Charles C. *Stanford White.* New York: Dodd, Mead, 1931. Reissued in paperback with an introduction by Paul Goldberger by Da Capo Press, New York, 1971.

Broderick, Mosette Glaser. "The Place Where Nobody Goes: McKim, Mead & White and the Development of the South Shore of Long Island" in *In Search of Modern Architecture.* New York: Architectural History Foundation and Cambridge, MA: MIT Press, 1982.

Downing, Antoinette F., and Vincent J. Scully, Jr. *The Architectural Heritage of Newport, Rhode Island,* second edition. New York: Clarkson N. Potter, 1967.

Ferree, Barr. *American Estates and Gardens.* New York: Munn & Co., 1904.

Lowe, David Garrard. *Stanford White's New York.* New York: Doubleday, 1992.

MacKay, Robert B., Anthony Barker, and Carol Traynor, eds. *Long Island Country Houses and Their Architects, 1860–1940.* New York: Society for the Preservation of Long Island Antiquities in Association with W. W. Norton & Co., 1997.

McKim, Mead & White. *A Monograph of the Work of McKim, Mead & White 1879–1915.* 4 vols. New York: The Architectural Book Publishing Co., 1915. Reissued in one volume, 1973.

Mesick, Cohen, Wilson-Baker, Architects. "The Isaac Bell House," Historic Structure Report (unpublished), 1995.

Moore, Charles. *The Life and Times of Charles Follen McKim.* Boston and New York: Houghton Mifflin Company, 1929.

Parrish Art Museum. *The Long Island Country House 1870–1930.* Southampton, NY: The Parrish Art Museum, 1988.

Roth, Leland. *The Architecture of McKim, Mead & White 1870–1920: A Building List.* New York and London: Garland Publishing Co., Inc., 1978.

Roth, Leland. *McKim, Mead & White, Architects.* New York: Harper & Row, 1983.

Scully, Vincent J., Jr. *The Shingle Style and the Stick Style: Architectural Theory and Design from Richardson to the Origins of Wright,* rev. ed. New Haven: Yale University Press, 1971.

Sheldon, George, ed. *Artistic Country Seats: Types of Recent American Villa and Cottage Architecture.* 1886.

Shopsin, William C., and Mosette Glaser Broderick. *The Villard Houses: Life Story of a Landmark.* New York: Viking Press in cooperation with the Municipal Art Society, 1990.

Waite, Diana S. *Stanford White's Venetian Room: Its Conception, Realization, & Restoration.* Albany, New York: Mount Ida Press in association with the Cultural Services of the French Embassy, 1998

Weinreb, Alan. "The History of the Lewis-Livingston-Mills Estate at Staatsburg," (unpublished).

White, Claire Nicolas, ed. *Stanford White: Letters to His Family.* New York: Rizzoli International Publications, 1997.

White, Lawrence Grant. *Sketches and Designs of Stanford White.* New York: The Architectural Book Publishing Co., 1920.

Wilson, Richard Guy. *McKim, Mead & White, Architects.* New York: Rizzoli International Publications, 1983.

# Index